Teaching about the Holocaust

A RESOURCE BOOK FOR EDUCATORS

United States Holocaust Memorial Museum, Washington, D.C.

I N T R O D U C T I O N

The United States Holocaust Memorial Museum is America's national institution for the documentation, study, and interpretation of Holocaust history, and serves as this country's memorial to the millions of people murdered during the Holocaust.

The Museum's primary mission is to inform Americans about this unprecedented tragedy; to commemorate those who suffered; and to inspire visitors to contemplate the moral implications of civic responsibilities.

Chartered by a unanimous Act of Congress in 1980 and located adjacent to the national Mall in Washington, D.C., the Museum strives to broaden public understanding of the history of the Holocaust through multifaceted programs: exhibitions; research and publication; collecting and preserving material evidence, art, and artifacts relating to the Holocaust; annual Holocaust commemorations known as Days of Remembrance; and a variety of public programming designed to enhance understanding of the Holocaust and related issues, including those of contemporary significance.

As mandated by Congress, the Museum has developed a number of resources, services, and programs to assist educators and students who want to teach and learn about the Holocaust, including this resource book. Please do not hesitate to contact us at the address or fax number below for further information.

U.S. Mail: Resource Center for Educators
          U. S. Holocaust Memorial Museum
          100 Raoul Wallenberg Place, SW
          Washington, DC 20024-2150

Electronic Mail: education@ushmm.org
Internet Address: <http://www.ushmm.org/>

Outreach Request Telephone Hotline: (202) 488-2661
Fax: (202) 488-6137

These concentration camp uniforms are displayed in the Museum's Permanent Exhibition.

MUSEUM INFORMATION FOR EDUCATORS

VISITING THE MUSEUM'S EXHIBITIONS

The Museum's **Permanent Exhibition** is recommended for visitors eleven years and older. This self-guided three-floor exhibition presents a comprehensive history of the Holocaust through artifacts, photographs, films, and eyewitness testimonies. Middle and high school students usually take between sixty and ninety minutes to walk through the exhibition; adults often take longer.

Individual Reservations: Timed passes are required only for the Permanent Exhibition. Same-day passes are distributed free of charge each day at the Museum beginning at 10:00 A.M. on a first-come, first-served basis. There is a limit of four passes per person. Advance passes may be acquired through *ProTix* for a small fee:

Washington area	(703) 218-6500	Elsewhere	(800) 400-9373
Baltimore area	(410) 481-6500		

ProTix also has a network of outlets in the Washington-Baltimore area. These outlets include all Waxie Maxie's, Record and Tape Traders, selected Safeway stores, the Wolf Trap Barns, and Office Outfitters.

Group Reservations: Groups of ten or more people must make group reservations; see pp. x–xi.

The Museum's special exhibition **Remember the Children** (Main floor) is recommended for visitors eight years and older. Daniel is a composite figure whose experiences are based on those of actual children. He survives to tell his story. The visit takes about thirty minutes and requires no special arrangements.

A second special exhibition **The Nazi Olympics** (Concourse level) documents the Nazi regime's exploitation of the 1936 Berlin Games for propaganda purposes. Photographs, films, and oral testimonies highlight the stories of Jewish athletes who boycotted or were excluded from the Games as well as those of Jewish and Black medalists. The visit takes about sixty minutes and requires no special arrangements. (Through July 1997.)

A third special exhibition **Schindler's List** (Concourse level) is recommended for visitors eleven years and older. The exhibition consists of photographs of Oskar Schindler and some of the Jews he helped, from the war period and later.

This poster, entitled Lost Childhoods, *is one of a set of nine posters developed by the Museum for classroom use.*

EDUCATIONAL RESOURCES AND PROGRAMS

Resource Center for Educators (Concourse level): The Center houses educational materials developed by the Museum and serves as a national repository for lesson plans, curricula, literature, and audio-visual material available nationwide. Files of current activities, organizations, and individuals in each state are provided to assist teachers in identifying local resources. The materials are available for preview and research during a visit to the Museum. Staff are available to assist educators with any questions. The Center is open 1 P.M. to 5 P.M. daily or by appointment.

Artifact Poster Set with Teacher Guide: The nine 3' x 2' color posters feature artifacts from the Museum's vast collection. Highlighted themes include the isolation of victims using identifying stars and badges; the role of technology (early computers) in locating victims; the ideology and practice of racial hygiene; the use of deception in deportations; examples of resistance and rescue. The set is available from the Museum Shop (202) 488-6144.

Tell Them We Remember: The Story of the Holocaust by Susan D. Bachrach (Little, Brown, 1994): The Museum reaches beyond its walls through this history of the Holocaust for young readers. Based on the Permanent Exhibition, it illustrates how the lives of more than twenty innocent children throughout Europe were affected by the tragedy. The author, a member of the Museum's staff, draws on the Museum's artifacts, photographs, maps, and oral histories of Holocaust survivors to recount the children's experiences as the story of the Holocaust unfolds. Includes chronology, bibliography, and glossary. Appropriate for parents and teachers to share with young readers. 128 pp. *Tell Them We Remember* is available from the Museum Shop (202-488-6144) or your local bookstore.

Annual National Conferences for Educators: Classroom teachers, administrators, and other educators have an opportunity to learn rationales, strategies, and approaches for teaching about the Holocaust from experienced practitioners and scholars. Conference sessions emphasize planning and implementing units of study. Participants meet with staff, visit Museum exhibitions, and receive a collection of educational materials.

Lukas Allenbaugh's Uncovering Dark Secrets *was a first-place winner in the Museum's 1994 national art contest.*

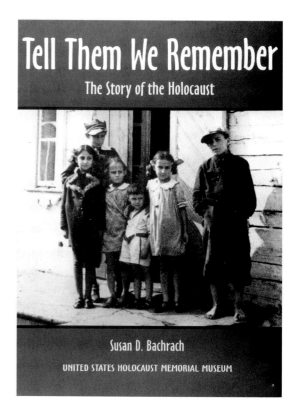

Teacher Training Workshops: These two- to three-day workshops are custom-designed specifically for smaller groups of teachers. Workshops are scheduled with the Museum's Coordinator of Teacher Training and are based on staff and space availability.

Presentations: The staff regularly conducts presentations at professional conferences and for community organizations on the educational programs of the Museum.

Annual National Writing and Art Contest: Each year the Museum sponsors a National Writing and Art Contest for junior high and high school students. The brochures are mailed out in late December and entries are due in late March. Winners are notified in May. First prize includes a trip to the Museum, and all winners and their school libraries receive books about the Holocaust and award certificates.

SPECIAL OUTREACH PROJECTS

Bringing the Lessons Home: Holocaust Education for the Community: In April 1994, the United States Holocaust Memorial Museum and the Fannie Mae Foundation announced a unique partnership with the Washington area community. Designed as an intensive program, this project focuses on understanding the history of the Holocaust and its implications for contemporary society. Throughout the school year, students and teachers tour the Museum, receive resource material, work in the interactive computer-based Learning Center, and attend workshops and in-depth classes at the Museum. In the summer, student interns from this project conduct tours for their peers, parents, and community groups. Participating teachers have an opportunity to share what they have learned at a national conference for educators. The project will expand over five years with aspects replicated on a national level.

Baltimore City School Project: With the support of the Flom Foundation, the Baltimore City Project will annually involve at least sixty educators and 1500 students who will learn about the history of the Holocaust through special programs at the Museum. This five-year project will also provide on-going assistance and special programs for Baltimore City educators.

GROUP VISIT INFORMATION AND GUIDELINES

◆ The Group Scheduling Office only accepts reservation requests *in writing*; no reservations can be made by telephone. Please send all requests to the attention of the Coordinator of Scheduling.

◆ A group is defined as ten or more people.

◆ Groups may request a reservation for any day of the week. Visits are scheduled on the half hour beginning at 10:00 A.M. and ending at 3:30 P.M.

◆ All requests must include your group's size and a specific date. By providing us with alternative dates, your chances of obtaining a reservation are greatly increased.

◆ Groups wishing to visit the Museum should send their request several months in advance. Requests are processed as early as six months ahead of the date requested, and we are happy to accept requests up to twelve months in advance. *All requests are filed according to date of receipt and booked on a first-come, first-served basis.*

◆ Groups including children or students below college level must be accompanied by chaperons. We require a ratio of one adult to every seven children because chaperons serve to provide guidance through difficult subject matter and to preserve order among their group in the event of an emergency.

◆ As a Federal institution, the Museum has a *special* policy on accepting reservations from any for-profit, third-party representatives (such as travel agents or tour operators). If you would like to know more about this policy, please call (202) 488-0455 to leave your address. We will be glad to send you the information outlining our policy.

◆ Please note: Weekends and holidays, as well as March–June and September–November, are extremely popular times to visit the Museum and Washington, D.C., in general. Because the Permanent Exhibition has a prescribed sequential path, we are concerned about space constraints, the quality of the individual visit, and the observance of fire and safety codes. Thus we have only a limited number of group spaces we may reserve at any given time. *If your group plans to attend during one of our busier periods, please include as many alternative dates as possible and submit your request as early as you can.*

The Group Scheduling Office's e-mail address is "group-visit@ushmm.org."

GROUP RESERVATION REQUEST FORM

UNITED STATES HOLOCAUST MEMORIAL MUSEUM

Please read carefully and fill out completely. Return at least four weeks prior to the date of your request. We will gladly accept requests up to one year in advance.

Group Name: _____

Contact Person: _____

Address: _____ Phone: _____

_____ FAX: _____

Date Requested _____ Time Range _____

Alternative Date 1 _____ Time Range _____

Alternative Date 2 _____ Time Range _____

* Due to high demand, many dates/times may be unavailable. Please indicate alternative or flexible times and dates, as they often significantly increase the likelihood of confirmation.

Number: _____ Adults _____ Children/Students _____

We require a ratio of at least one adult to every seven children/students below college level.

If your group is confirmed by the Scheduling Office, you may request to meet with a staff member for a 15–30 minute debriefing session after a group visit. Please send your request to the attention of the Education Department or fax (202) 314-7888. Please note that these programs are dependent upon the availability of staff. *These services are unavailable to those groups booked by third parties.*

Please send this form to: Coordinator of Scheduling
U.S. Holocaust Memorial Museum
100 Raoul Wallenberg Place, SW
Washington, DC 20024-2150
FAX (202) 488-2606

This form represents a *request* for a group appointment; it does not guarantee a booking. Separate confirmation packets are sent via U.S. Mail.

GUIDELINES FOR TEACHING ABOUT THE HOLOCAUST

Why Teach Holocaust History?

The history of the Holocaust represents one of the most effective, and most extensively documented, subjects for a pedagogical examination of basic moral issues. A structured inquiry into Holocaust history yields critical lessons for an investigation of human behavior. A study of the Holocaust also addresses one of the central tenets of education in the United States, which is to examine what it means to be a responsible citizen. Through a study of the Holocaust, students can come to realize that:

◆ democratic institutions and values are not automatically sustained but need to be appreciated, nurtured, and protected;

◆ silence and indifference to the suffering of others, or to the infringement of civil rights in any society, can—however unintentionally—serve to perpetuate the problems; and

◆ the Holocaust was not an accident in history—it occurred because individuals, organizations, and governments made choices that not only legalized discrimination but that allowed prejudice, hatred, and ultimately mass murder to occur.

Questions of Rationale

Because the objective of teaching any subject is to engage the intellectual curiosity of the student in order to inspire critical thought and personal growth, it is helpful to structure your lesson plan on the Holocaust by considering throughout questions of rationale. Before addressing what and how to teach, we would recommend that you contemplate the following:

◆ Why should students learn this history?

◆ What are the most significant lessons students can learn about the Holocaust?

◆ Why is a particular reading, image, document, or film an appropriate medium for conveying the lessons about the Holocaust that you wish to teach?

Among the various rationales offered by educators who have incorporated a study of the Holocaust into their various courses and disciplines are these:

◆ The Holocaust was a watershed event, not only in the 20th century but in the entire history of humanity.

◆ Study of the Holocaust assists students in developing understanding of the ramifications of prejudice, racism, and stereotyping in any society. It helps students develop an awareness of the value of pluralism, and encourages tolerance of diversity in a pluralistic society.

◆ The Holocaust provides a context for exploring the dangers of remaining silent, apathetic, and indifferent in the face of others' oppression.

◆ Holocaust history demonstrates how a modern nation can utilize its technological expertise and bureaucratic infrastructure to implement destructive policies ranging from social engineering to genocide.

◆ A study of the Holocaust helps students think about the use and abuse of power, and the role and responsibilities of individuals, organizations, and nations when confronted with civil rights violations and/or policies of genocide.

◆ As students gain insight into the many historical, social, religious, political, and economic factors which cumulatively resulted in the Holocaust, they gain a perspective on how history happens and how a convergence of factors can contribute to the disintegration of civilized values. Part of one's responsibility as a citizen in a democracy is to learn to identify the danger signals, and to know when to react.

When you, as an educator, take the time to consider the rationale for your lesson on the Holocaust, you will be more likely to select content that speaks to your students' interests and that provides them with a clearer understanding of the history. Most students demonstrate a high level of interest in studying the Holocaust precisely because the subject raises questions of fairness, justice, individual identity, peer pressure, conformity, indifference, and obedience— issues that adolescents confront in their daily lives. Students are also struck by the magnitude of the Holocaust, and by the fact that so many people acting as collaborators, perpetrators, and bystanders allowed this genocide to occur by failing to protest or resist.

Students in grades 7 and above demonstrate an ability to empathize with individual eyewitness accounts as well as begin to grasp the complexities of the history, including the scope and scale of the events. While elementary students are able to empathize with individual survivor accounts, they often have difficulty placing these personal stories in a larger historical context. Such demonstrable developmental differences have traditionally shaped social studies curricula throughout the country; in most states, students are not introduced to European history and geography—the context for the Holocaust—before grades 7 or 8.

Methodological Considerations

1. DEFINE WHAT YOU MEAN BY "HOLOCAUST."

The Holocaust refers to a specific event in 20th-century history: the state-sponsored, systematic persecution and annihilation of European Jewry by Nazi Germany and its collaborators between 1933 and 1945. Jews were the primary victims—six million were murdered; Gypsies, the handicapped, and Poles were also targeted for destruction or decimation for racial, ethnic, or national reasons. Millions more, including homosexuals, Jehovah's Witnesses, Soviet prisoners of war, and political dissidents, also suffered grievous oppression and death under Nazi tyranny.

2. AVOID COMPARISONS OF PAIN.

A study of the Holocaust should always highlight the different policies carried out by the Nazi regime toward various groups of people; however, these distinctions should not be presented as a basis for comparison of suffering between them. Avoid generalizations which suggest exclusivity, such as "the victims of the Holocaust suffered the most cruelty ever faced by a people in the history of humanity." One cannot presume that the horror of an individual, family, or community destroyed by the Nazis was any greater than that experienced by victims of other genocides.

3. AVOID SIMPLE ANSWERS TO COMPLEX HISTORY.

A study of the Holocaust raises difficult questions about human behavior, and it often involves complicated answers as to why events occurred. Be wary of over-simplifications. Allow students to contemplate the various factors that contributed to the Holocaust; do not attempt to reduce Holocaust history to one or two catalysts in isolation from the other factors that came into play. For example, the Holocaust was not simply the logical and inevitable consequence of unbridled racism. Rather, racism, combined with centuries-old bigotry, renewed by a nationalistic fervor which emerged in Europe in the latter half of the 19th century, fueled by Germany's defeat in World War I and its national humiliation following the Treaty of Versailles, exacerbated by worldwide economic hard times, the ineffectiveness of the Weimar Republic, and international indifference, and catalyzed by the political charisma, militaristic inclusiveness, and manipulative propaganda of Adolf Hitler's Nazi regime, contributed to the eventuality of the Holocaust.

4. JUST BECAUSE IT HAPPENED DOES NOT MEAN IT WAS INEVITABLE.

Too often students have the simplistic impression that the Holocaust was inevitable. Just because an historical event took place, and it was documented in textbooks and on film, does not mean that it had to happen. This seemingly obvious concept is often overlooked by students and teachers alike. The Holocaust took place because individuals, groups, and nations made decisions to act or not to act. By focusing on those decisions, we gain insight into history and human nature, and we can better help our students to become critical thinkers.

5. Strive for precision of language.

Any study of the Holocaust touches upon nuances of human behavior. Because of the complexity of the history, there is a temptation to overgeneralize and thus to distort the facts (e.g., "all concentration camps were killing centers" or "all Germans were collaborators"). Rather, teachers must strive to help students distinguish between categories of behavior and relevant historical references; to clarify the differences between prejudice and discrimination, collaborators and bystanders, armed and spiritual resistance, direct orders and assumed orders, concentration camps and killing centers, and guilt and responsibility.

Words that describe human behavior often have multiple meanings. Resistance, for example, usually refers to a physical act of armed revolt. During the Holocaust, it also meant partisan activism that ranged from smuggling messages, food, and weapons to actual military engagement. But resistance also embraced willful disobedience: continuing to practice religious and cultural traditions in defiance of the rules; creating fine art, music, and poetry inside ghettos and concentration camps. For many, simply maintaining the will to remain alive in the face of abject brutality was the surest act of spiritual resistance.

6. Make careful distinctions about sources of information.

Students need practice in distinguishing between fact, opinion, and fiction; between primary and secondary sources; and between types of evidence such as court testimonies, oral histories, and other written documents. Hermeneutics—the science of interpretation—should be called into play to help guide your students in their analysis of sources. Students should be encouraged to consider why a particular text was written, who the intended audience was, whether there were any biases inherent in the information, any gaps in discussion, whether gaps in certain passages were inadvertent or not, and how the information has been used to interpret various events.

Because scholars often base their research on different bodies of information, varying interpretations of history can emerge. Consequently, all interpretations are subject to analytical evaluation. Only by refining their own "hermeneutic of suspicion" can students mature into readers who discern the difference between legitimate scholars who present competing historical interpretations and those who distort or deny historical fact for personal or political gain.

7. TRY TO AVOID STEREOTYPICAL DESCRIPTIONS.

Though all Jews were targeted for destruction by the Nazis, the experiences of all Jews were not the same. Simplistic views and stereotyping take place when groups of people are viewed as monolithic in attitudes and actions. How ethnic groups or social clusters are labeled and portrayed in school curricula has a direct impact on how students perceive groups in their daily lives. Remind your students that, although members of a group may share common experiences and beliefs, generalizations about them, without benefit of modifying or qualifying terms (e.g., "sometimes," "usually," "in many cases but not all") tend to stereotype group behavior and distort historical reality. Thus, all Germans cannot be characterized as Nazis, nor should any nationality be reduced to a singular or one-dimensional description.

8. DO NOT ROMANTICIZE HISTORY TO ENGAGE STUDENTS' INTEREST.

One of the great risks of Holocaust education is the danger of fostering cynicism in our students by exposing them to the worst of human nature. Regardless, accuracy of fact must be a teacher's priority. People who risked their lives to rescue victims of Nazi oppression provide useful and important role models for students, yet an overemphasis on heroic tales in a unit on the Holocaust results in an inaccurate and unbalanced account of the history. It is important to bear in mind that only a small fraction of non-Jews under Nazi occupation helped to rescue Jews.

9. CONTEXTUALIZE THE HISTORY YOU ARE TEACHING.

Events of the Holocaust, and particularly how individuals and organizations behaved at that time, must be placed in a historical context so that students can begin to comprehend the circumstances that encouraged or discouraged these acts. Frame your approach to specific events and acts of complicity or defiance by considering when and where an act took place; the immediate consequences to oneself and one's family of assisting victims; the impact of contemporaneous events; the degree of control the Nazis had on a country or local population; the cultural attitudes of particular native populations historically toward different victim groups; and the availability, effectiveness, and risk of potential hiding places.

Students should be reminded that individuals and groups do not always fit neatly into the same categories of behavior. The very same people did not always act consistently as "bystanders," "collaborators," "perpetrators," or "rescuers." Individuals and groups often behaved differently depending upon changing events and circumstances. The same person who in 1933 might have stood by and remained uninvolved while witnessing social discrimination of Jews might later have joined up with the SA and become a collaborator or have been moved to dissent vocally or act in defense of Jewish friends and neighbors.

Encourage your students not to categorize groups of people only on the basis of their experiences during the Holocaust: contextualization is critical so that victims are not perceived only as victims. Although Jews were the central victims of the Nazi regime, they had a vibrant culture and long history in Europe prior to the Nazi era. By exposing students to some of the cultural contributions and achievements of two thousand years of European Jewish life, you help students to balance their perception of Jews as victims and to better appreciate the traumatic disruption in Jewish history caused by the Holocaust.

Similarly, students may know very little about Gypsies except for the negative images and derogatory descriptions promulgated by the Nazis. Students would benefit from a broader viewpoint, learning something about Gypsy history and culture and understanding the diverse ways of life among different Gypsy groups.

10. TRANSLATE STATISTICS INTO PEOPLE.

In any study of the Holocaust, the sheer number of victims challenges easy comprehension. Teachers need to show that individual people are behind the statistics, comprised of families of grandparents, parents, and children. First-person accounts and memoir literature provide students with a way of making meaning out of collective numbers. Although students should be careful about overgeneralizing from first-person accounts such as those from survivors, journalists, relief workers, bystanders, and liberators, personal accounts help students get beyond statistics and make historical events of the Holocaust more immediate.

11. BE SENSITIVE TO APPROPRIATE WRITTEN AND AUDIO-VISUAL CONTENT.

One of the primary concerns of educators is how to introduce students to the horrors of the Holocaust. Graphic material should be used in a judicious manner and only to the extent necessary to achieve the objective of the lesson. Teachers should remind themselves that each student and each class is different, and that what seems appropriate for one may not be for all.

Students are essentially a "captive audience." When we assault them with images of horror for which they are unprepared, we violate a basic trust: the obligation of a teacher to provide a "safe" learning environment. The assumption that all students will seek to understand human behavior after being exposed to horrible images is fallacious. Some students may be so appalled by images of brutality and mass murder that they are discouraged from studying the subject further; others may become fascinated in a more voyeuristic fashion, subordinating further critical analysis of the history to the superficial titillation of looking at images of starvation, disfigurement, and death. Many events and deeds that occurred within the context of the Holocaust do not rely for their depiction directly on the graphic horror of mass killings or other barbarisms. It is recommended that images and texts that do not exploit either the victims' memories or the students' emotional vulnerability form the centerpiece of Holocaust curricula.

12. STRIVE FOR BALANCE IN ESTABLISHING WHOSE PERSPECTIVE INFORMS YOUR STUDY OF THE HOLOCAUST.

Often, too great an emphasis is placed on the victims of Nazi aggression rather than on the victimizers who forced people to make impossible choices or simply left them with no choice to make. Most students express empathy for victims of mass murder. But it is not uncommon for students to assume that the victims may have done something to justify the actions against them, and thus to place inappropriate blame on the victims themselves.

There is also a tendency among students to glorify power, even when it is used to kill innocent people. Many teachers indicate that their students are intrigued and, in some cases, intellectually seduced by the symbols of power which pervaded Nazi propaganda (e.g., the swastika; Nazi flags and regalia; Nazi slogans, rituals, and music). Rather than highlight the trappings of Nazi power, teachers should ask students to evaluate how such elements are used by governments (including our own) to build, protect, and mobilize a society. Students should be encouraged to contemplate as well how such elements can be abused and manipulated by governments to implement and legitimize acts of terror and even genocide.

In any review of the propaganda used to promote Nazi ideology, Nazi stereotypes of targeted victim groups, and the Hitler regime's justifications for persecution and murder, teachers need to remind students that just because such policies and beliefs are under discussion in class does not mean they are acceptable. It would be a terrible irony if students arrived at such a conclusion.

Furthermore, any study of the Holocaust should address both the victims and the perpetrators of violence and attempt to portray each as human beings, capable of moral judgment and independent decision-making but challenged by circumstances which made both self-defense and independent thought not merely difficult but perilous and potentially lethal.

13. SELECT APPROPRIATE LEARNING ACTIVITIES.

Just because students favor a certain learning activity does not necessarily mean that it should be used. For example, such activities as word scrambles, crossword puzzles, and other gimmicky exercises tend not to encourage critical analysis but lead instead to low level types of thinking and, in the case of Holocaust curricula, trivialize the importance of studying this history. When the effects of a particular activity run counter to the rationale for studying the history, then that activity should not be used.

Similarly, activities that encourage students to construct models of killing camps should also be reconsidered since any assignment along this line will almost inevitably end up being simplistic, time-consuming, and tangential to the educational objectives for studying the history of the Holocaust.

Thought-provoking learning activities are preferred, but even here, there are pitfalls to avoid. In studying complex human behavior, many teachers rely upon simulation exercises meant to help students "experience" unfamiliar situations. Even when teachers take great care to prepare a class for such an activity, simulating experiences from the Holocaust remains pedagogically unsound. The activity may engage students, but they often forget the purpose of the lesson and, even worse, they are left with the impression at the conclusion of the activity that they now know what it was like during the Holocaust. Holocaust survivors and eyewitnesses are among the first to indicate the grave difficulty of finding words to describe their experiences. Even more revealing, they argue the virtual impossibility of trying to simulate accurately what it was like to live on a daily basis with fear, hunger, disease, unfathomable loss, and the unrelenting threat of abject brutality and death.

The problem with trying to simulate situations from the Holocaust is that complex events and actions are oversimplified, and students are left with a skewed view of history. Since there are numerous primary source accounts, both written and visual, as well as survivors and eyewitnesses who can describe actual choices faced and made by individuals, groups, and nations during this period, teachers should draw upon these resources and refrain from simulation games that lead to a trivialization of the subject matter.

If they are not attempting to recreate situations from the Holocaust, simulation activities can be used effectively, especially when they have been designed to explore varying aspects of human behavior such as fear, scapegoating, conflict resolution, and difficult decision-making. Asking students in the course of a discussion, or as part of a writing assignment, to consider various perspectives on a particular event or historical experience is fundamentally different from involving a class in a simulation game.

14. REINFORCE THE OBJECTIVES OF YOUR LESSON PLAN.

As in all teaching situations, the opening and closing lessons are critically important. A strong opening should serve to dispel misinformation students may have prior to studying the Holocaust. It should set a reflective tone, move students from passive to active learners, indicate to students that their ideas and opinions matter, and establish that this history has multiple ramifications for themselves as individuals and as members of society as a whole.

A strong closing should emphasize synthesis by encouraging students to connect this history to other world events as well as the world they live in today. Students should be encouraged to reflect on what they have learned and to consider what this study means to them personally and as citizens of a democracy. Most importantly, your closing lesson should encourage further examination of Holocaust history, literature, and art.

Incorporating a Study of the Holocaust into Existing Courses

The Holocaust can be effectively integrated into various existing courses within the school curriculum. This section presents sample rationale statements and methodological approaches for incorporating a study of the Holocaust in seven different courses. Each course synopsis constitutes a mere fraction of the various rationales and approaches currently used by educators. Often, the rationales and methods listed under one course can be applied as well to other courses.

UNITED STATES HISTORY

Although the history of the United States is introduced at various grade levels throughout most school curricula, all states require students to take a course in United States history at the high school level. Including a study of the Holocaust into U.S. History courses can encourage students to:

◆ examine the dilemmas that arise when foreign policy goals are narrowly defined, as solely in terms of the national interest, thus denying the validity of universal moral and human priorities;

◆ understand what happens when parliamentary democratic institutions fail;

◆ examine the responses of governmental and non-governmental organizations in the United States to the plight of Holocaust victims (e.g., the Evian Conference, the debate over the Wagner-Rogers bill to assist refugee children, the ill-fated voyage of the S.S. *St. Louis*, the Emergency Rescue Committee, the rallies and efforts of Rabbi Stephen S. Wise, and the decision by the U.S. not to bomb the railroad lines leading into Auschwitz);

◆ explore the role of American and Allied soldiers in liberating victims from Nazi concentration camps and killing centers, using, for example, first-person accounts of liberators to ascertain their initial responses to, and subsequent reflections about, what they witnessed; and

◆ examine the key role played by the U.S. in bringing Nazi perpetrators to trial at Nuremberg and in other war crimes trials.

Since most history and social studies teachers in the United States rely upon standard textbooks, they can incorporate the Holocaust into regular units of study such as the Great Depression, World War II, and the Cold War. Questions that introduce Holocaust studies into these subject areas include:

The Great Depression: How did the U.S. respond to the Depression? How were U.S. electoral politics influenced by the Depression? What were the immediate consequences of the Depression on the European economic and political system established by the Versailles Treaty of 1919? What was the impact of the Depression upon the electoral strength of the Nazi party in Germany? Was the Depression a contributing factor to the Nazis' rise to power?

World War II: What was the relationship between the U.S. and Nazi Germany from 1933 to 1939? How did the actions of Nazi Germany influence U.S. foreign policy? What was the response of the U.S. Government and non-governmental organizations to the unfolding events of the Holocaust? What was the role of the U.S. in the war crimes trials?

The Cold War: How did the rivalries between the World War II allies influence American attitudes toward former Nazis? What was the position of America's European allies toward members of the former Nazi regime?

WORLD HISTORY

Although various aspects of world history are incorporated throughout school curricula, most students are not required to take World History courses. It is in the context of World History courses, however, that the Holocaust is generally taught. Inclusion of the Holocaust in a World History course helps students to:

◆ examine events, deeds, and ideas in European history that contributed to the Holocaust, such as the history of antisemitism in Europe, 19th-century race science, the rise of German nationalism, the defeat of Germany in World War I, and the failure of the Weimar Republic to govern successfully;

◆ reflect upon the idea that civilization has been progressing [one possible exercise might be to have students develop a definition of "civilization" in class, and then have them compare and contrast Nazi claims for the "Thousand-Year Reich" with the actual policies they employed to realize that vision; the dissonance raised in such a lesson helps students to see that government policies can encompass evil, particularly when terror and brute force crush dissent];

◆ explore how the various policies of the Nazi regime were interrelated (e.g., the connections between establishing a totalitarian government, carrying out racial policies, and waging war); and

◆ reflect upon the moral and ethical implications of the Nazi era as a watershed in world history (e.g., the systematic planning and implementation of a government policy to kill millions of people; the use of technological advances to carry out mass slaughter; the role of Nazi collaborators; and the role of bystanders around the world who chose not to intervene in the persecution and murder of Jews and other victims).

Once again, since most teachers of European history rely upon standard text-books and a chronological approach, teachers may wish to incorporate the Holocaust into the following, standardized units of study in European History: The Aftermath of World War I; The Rise of Dictators; The World at War, 1939–45; and The Consequences of War. Questions which introduce Holocaust studies into these subject areas include:

The Aftermath of World War I: What role did the Versailles Treaty play in the restructuring of European and world politics? How did the reconfiguration of Europe following World War I influence German national politics in the period 1919–33?

The Rise of the Dictators: What factors led to the rise of totalitarian regimes in Europe in the period between the two world wars? How was antisemitism used by the Nazis and other regimes (Hungary, Romania, U.S.S.R.) to justify totalitarian measures?

The World at War, 1939–45: Why has the Holocaust often been called a "war within the war?" How did the Holocaust affect Nazi military decisions? Why might it be "easier" to commit genocidal acts during wartime than during a period of relative peace?

The Consequences of War: What was the connection between World War II and the formation of the State of Israel? Was a new strain of international morality introduced with the convening of the Nuremberg Tribunals? How did the Cold War affect the fate of former Nazis?

WORLD CULTURES

A course on World Cultures incorporates knowledge from both the humanities and the social sciences into a study of cultural patterns and social institutions of various societies. A study of the Holocaust in a World Cultures course helps students:

◆ examine conflicts arising between majority and minority groups in a specific cultural sphere (Europe between 1933 and 1945);

◆ further their understanding of how a government can use concepts such as culture, ethnicity, race, diversity, and nationality as weapons to persecute, murder, and annihilate people;

◆ analyze the extent to which cultures are able to survive and maintain their traditions and institutions when faced with threats to their very existence (e.g., retaining religious practices, recording eyewitness accounts, and hiding cultural symbols and artifacts); and

◆ apply understandings gleaned from an examination of the Holocaust to genocides which have occurred in other cultural spheres.

GOVERNMENT

Government courses at the high school level usually focus on understanding the U.S. political system, comparative studies of various governments, and the international relationship of nations. The Holocaust can be incorporated into a study of government in order to demonstrate how the development of public policy can become directed to genocidal ends when dissent and debate are silenced. Inclusion of Holocaust studies in Government courses helps students:

◆ compare governmental systems (e.g., by investigating how the Weimar Constitution in Germany prior to the Nazi seizure of power was similar to, or different from, the Constitution of the United States; by comparing the Nazi system of governance with that of the United States);

◆ study the process of how a state can degenerate from a (parliamentary) democracy into a totalitarian state (e.g., by examining the processes by which the Nazis gained absolute control of the German government and how the Nazi government then controlled virtually all segments of German society);

◆ examine how the development of public policy can lead to genocidal ends, especially when people remain silent in the face of discriminatory practices (e.g., the development of Nazi racial and genocide policies towards Jews and other victim groups beginning with the philosophical platform elaborated in Hitler's *Mein Kampf*, continuing through the state-imposed Nuremberg Laws, and culminating with governmental policies of murder and extermination after 1941);

◆ examine the role of Nazi bureaucracy in implementing policies of murder and annihilation (e.g., the development and maintenance of a system to identify, isolate, deport, enslave, and kill targeted people, and then redistribute their remaining belongings);

◆ examine the role of various individuals in the rise and fall of a totalitarian government (e.g., those who supported Nazi Germany, those who were passive, and those who resisted, both internally, such as partisans and others who carried out revolts, and externally, such as the Allies); and

◆ recognize that among the legacies of the Holocaust have been the creation of the United Nations in 1945 and its ongoing efforts to develop and adopt numerous, significant human rights bills (e.g., the U.N. Declaration of Human Rights and the U.N. Convention on Genocide).

CONTEMPORARY WORLD PROBLEMS

Many schools include a Contemporary World Problems course at the senior high level which allows students to conduct an in-depth study of a topic such as genocide. The focus is usually on what constitutes genocide, and areas of investigation include various preconditions, patterns, consequences, and methods of intervention and prevention of genocide. A study of the Holocaust in Contemporary World Problems curricula can help students to:

◆ comprehend the similarities and differences between governmental policies during the Holocaust and contemporary policies that create the potential for ethnocide or genocide (e.g., comparing and contrasting the philosophy and/or policies of the Nazi regime with that of the Khmer Rouge in Cambodia);

◆ compare and contrast the world response of governments and non-governmental organizations to the Holocaust with the responses of governments and non-governmental organizations to mass killings today (e.g., comparing the decisions made at the Evian Conference in 1938 to the U.S. response to the Cambodian genocide between 1974 and 1979, or the response of non-governmental organizations like the International Red Cross to the Nazi genocide of Jews during the Holocaust with that of Amnesty International to political killings in Argentina, Guatemala, Indonesia, and Cambodia in contemporary times); and

◆ analyze the relationship of the Holocaust and its legacy to the formation of the State of Israel.

LITERATURE

Literature is read in English classes across grade levels and is also used to enhance and strengthen social studies and science courses. The literature curriculum is generally organized thematically or around categories such as American Literature, British Literature, European Literature, and World Literature. Literature is capable of providing thought-provoking perspectives on a myriad of subjects and concerns that can engage students in ways that standard textbooks and essays do not.

Holocaust literature encompasses a variety of literary genres including novels, short stories, drama, poetry, diaries, and memoirs. This broad spectrum gives teachers a wide range of curriculum choices. Because Holocaust literature derives from a true-to-life epic in human history, its stories reveal basic truths about human nature and provide adolescent readers with credible models of heroism and dignity. At the same time, it compels them to confront the reality of the human capacity for evil.

Because so many of the stories intersect with issues in students' own lives, Holocaust literature can inspire a commitment to reject indifference to human suffering and can instruct them about relevant social issues such as the effects of intolerance and elitism. Studying literary responses to the Holocaust helps students:

◆ develop a deeper respect for human decency by asking them to confront the moral depravity and the extent of Nazi evil (e.g., the abject cruelty of the Nazi treatment of victims even prior to the round-ups and deportations, the event of *Kristallnacht*, the deportations in boxcars, the mass killings, and the so-called medical experiments of Nazi doctors);

◆ recognize the deeds of heroism demonstrated by teenagers and adults in ghettos and concentration camps (e.g., the couriers who smuggled messages, goods, and weapons in and out of the Warsaw ghetto; the partisans who used arms to resist the Nazis; and the uprisings and revolts in various ghettos including Warsaw and in killing centers such as Treblinka);

◆ explore the spiritual resistance evidenced in literary responses which portray the irrepressible dignity of people who transcended the evil of their murderers, as found for example in the clandestine writing of diaries, poetry, and plays;

◆ recognize the different roles that were assumed or thrust upon people during the Holocaust, such as victim, oppressor, bystander, and rescuer;

◆ examine the moral choices, or absence of choices, that were confronted by both young and old, victim and perpetrator; and

◆ analyze the corruption of language cultivated by the Nazis, particularly in the use of euphemisms to mask their evil intent (e.g., their use of the terms "emigration" for expulsion, "evacuation" for deportation, "deportation" for transportation to concentration camps and killing centers, "police actions" for round-ups that typically led to mass murder, and "Final Solution" for the planned annihilation of every Jew in Europe).

ART AND ART HISTORY

One of the goals for studying art history is to enable students to understand the role of art in society. The Holocaust can be incorporated into a study of art and art history to illuminate how the Nazis used art for propagandistic purposes and how victims used artistic expression to communicate their protest, despair, and/or hope. A study of art during the Holocaust helps students:

◆ analyze the motivations for, and implications of, the Nazis' censorship activities in the fine and literary arts, theater, and music (e.g., the banning of books and certain styles of painting and the May 1933 book burnings);

◆ examine the values and beliefs of the Nazis and how the regime perceived the world by, for example, examining Nazi symbols of power, Nazi propaganda posters, paintings, and drawings deemed "acceptable" rather than "degenerate";

◆ study how people living under Nazi control used art as a form of resistance (e.g., examining the extent to which the victims created art, the dangers they faced in doing so, the various forms of art that were created and the settings in which they were created, and the diversity of themes and content in this artistic expression);

◆ examine art created by Holocaust victims and survivors and explore its capacity to document diverse experiences, including life prior to the Holocaust, life inside the ghettos, the deportations, and the myriad experiences in the concentration camp system; and

◆ examine interpretations of the Holocaust as expressed in contemporary art, art exhibitions, and memorials.

ANNOTATED BIBLIOGRAPHY

The purpose of this annotated bibliography is to help teachers choose from the vast array of Holocaust literature books that might be useful to them and to their students. This bibliography is not meant to indicate that these are the best examples of Holocaust literature, although they are all excellent books. The works cited here were selected both because of individual merit and specifically because they address particular aspects of Holocaust experience. Together, these books attempt to encompass the tremendous scope of this historical period.

We have tried, for the most part, to include books that are readily available and, where possible, available in paperback. A few books that were out of print at the time this bibliography was compiled have nevertheless been included simply because they are too important to be omitted.

The difficulty in compiling a selective list of Holocaust literature is complicated not only by the great amount of material available but by the subject matter itself. The Holocaust was a monumental event in history. It involved millions of people in dozens of nations, and its effects were felt in every aspect of their lives. There is, therefore, no simple answer to the questions, "What's the best book for me to read about the Holocaust?" or "If I can only read one or two books, which ones should they be?" Any one book can present only a partial perspective. Where a good general history of the period can provide historical background, a personal narrative will translate that history into human terms, and a more specialized history will examine a particular aspect of that history in greater depth.

Which book or books you should read will depend both on how much time you are able to commit and on the aspect of the Holocaust upon which you are focusing. No one can learn, or teach, everything about the Holocaust. First, determine your goals, and then select the most appropriate materials. A broad range of materials have been included on these lists to represent the scope of the Holocaust and to enable teachers to select the materials best suited to their individual approaches to the subject.

The lists are presented in three sections organized by reading level: middle school, high school, and adult. Almost without exception, the titles on the middle school lists are books that were originally published by the children's book divisions of publishing houses, indicating that the intended audience was young people aged fourteen or under. In many cases, however, that range can be expanded upward. Although a few of the books on the high school list were published with a "young adult" audience in mind, most of them are adult books that are particularly well suited to high school students. A number of titles have been included again on the adult list; all of the books on the high school list, however, are also recommended for adult readers. (At the end of this bibliography is an alphabetized index by author to all the volumes included in this list.)

In selecting books for student use, it is as important to determine when a book should be assigned as it is to decide which book to use. Most students have little prior knowledge of the history of this period and, therefore, need some historical background to be able to put the book they are reading into perspective. This is especially true of the fiction and personal narratives on the middle school list. Many of these books were written from a child's perspective; the child in the book frequently does not really understand the events he or she is caught up in, and neither will the reader without some historical background.

As new Holocaust literature is constantly appearing, it is also important to establish criteria for examining these materials. In addition to the usual standards of literary quality and historical accuracy, two phrases from Lawrence L. Langer's *The Age of Atrocity: Death in Modern Literature* set the parameters in this arena. At one end of the scale, the book should be one that actually confronts the horrors of the Holocaust; it should not "circumspectly [skirt] the horror implicit in the theme but [leave] the reader with the mournful if psychologically unburdened feeling that he has had a genuine encounter with inappropriate death." At the other extreme, too great a concentration on the horrors, especially if presented with graphic details, tends to overwhelm the reader and numb the senses; Langer refers to these works as "mere catalogues of atrocities." Between these two extremes, there is a wealth of material, only a fraction of which is listed here, that will enable students and teachers to confront the Holocaust and the issues that it raises.

Middle School   1. HISTORY, GENERAL

Altshuler, David A. *Hitler's War Against the Jews—the Holocaust: A Young Reader's Version of* The War Against the Jews 1933–1945 *by Lucy Dawidowicz.* West Orange, NJ: Behrman House, 1978.

Altshuler follows Dawidowicz's text closely but shortens and simplifies it for younger readers. This is an excellent introductory overview to the history of the Holocaust.

Middle School
(cont.)

Bachrach, Susan D. *Tell Them We Remember: The Story of the Holocaust.* Boston: Little, Brown, 1994.

Bachrach tells the story of the Holocaust as presented in the United States Holocaust Memorial Museum in brief, thematic segments illustrated by artifacts and historical photographs. Sidebars tell the personal stories of more than twenty young people of various social and religious backgrounds and nationalities who suffered or died during the Holocaust.

Chaikin, Miriam. *A Nightmare in History: The Holocaust 1933–1945.* Boston: Houghton Mifflin, 1987.

The author effectively weaves personal narratives into this concise, readable history. She presents the facts clearly and succinctly but never allows the reader to forget the faces behind the facts.

Meltzer, Milton. *Never to Forget: The Jews of the Holocaust.* New York: Dell Publishing Company, 1977.

Meltzer's history focuses on the Jewish perspective on the Holocaust, including brief histories of antisemitism and of Jewish resistance. One of the first books on the Holocaust written for young people, this is still one of the most useful.

Rogasky, Barbara. *Smoke and Ashes: The Story of the Holocaust.* New York: Holiday House, 1988.

Blending a narrative of historical events with personal testimonies, Rogasky poses these questions: How did the Holocaust happen and why? Couldn't anyone stop it? How could the Jews let it happen? She includes a chapter on non-Jewish victims.

Rossell, Seymour. *The Holocaust: The Fire that Raged.* New York: Franklin Watts, 1990.

In clear and simple prose, Rossell chronicles events from the rise of Nazism through the ghettos, the camps, rescue, and resistance, to the Nuremberg and Eichmann trials. This is good introductory or reference material for those unfamiliar with the historical events.

Middle School
(cont.)

2. HISTORY, SPECIALIZED

Abells, Chana. *Children We Remember*. New York: Greenwillow, 1986.

Graphic black-and-white photographs from the collection at Yad Vashem convey, in terms more powerful than words ever could, the fate of European Jewish children, from their life before the Nazis through the various stages of Nazi rule.

Friedman, Ina R. *The Other Victims: First-Person Stories of Non-Jews Persecuted by the Nazis*. Boston: Houghton Mifflin, 1990.

This is the only work written to date for young people that focuses on non-Jewish victims of the Holocaust. Friedman interviews Gypsies, Jehovah's Witnesses and other religious figures, the disabled, and members of other victim groups. Information is included on blacks and gays, although she was unable to provide interviews.

Landau, Elaine. *Warsaw Ghetto Uprising*. New York: Macmillan, 1992.

After briefly describing the creation of the Warsaw ghetto, the author concentrates on the 28 days of the uprising. Both text and photographs are graphic at times but only to the extent necessary to describe the events accurately.

Meltzer, Milton. *Rescue: The Story of How Gentiles Saved Jews in the Holocaust*. New York: HarperCollins Children's Books, 1991.

This work focuses on the non-Jews who risked their lives to save Jews throughout Nazi-occupied Europe. The author uses material excerpted from diaries and letters, personal interviews, and eyewitness accounts.

Stadtler, Bea. *The Holocaust: A History of Courage and Resistance*. West Orange, NJ: Behrman House, 1975.

One of the first Holocaust books written for young people, this work focuses on Jewish resistance. This is a good companion to Meltzer's *Rescue*; together the two books present an excellent picture of both Jewish and non-Jewish resistance.

Middle School
(cont.)

3. BIOGRAPHY

Atkinson, Linda. *In Kindling Flame: The Story of Hannah Senesh 1921–1944*. New York: William Morrow, 1992.

Atkinson combines history and biography in this story of the noted Jewish-Hungarian resistance fighter. Because the author includes an account of Senesh's capture and execution, as well as the historical background essential for full understanding of her story, this book can either complement Senesh's diary or serve as an alternative for younger readers.

Bernheim, Mark. *Father of the Orphans: The Story of Janusz Korczak*. New York: Dutton Children's Books, 1989.

Much of this moving biography deals with Korczak's life before the Holocaust. In illuminating his character, the book provides the reader with a context in which to place his devotion to the children in his orphanage and his decision to accompany them to the Treblinka death camp.

Friedman, Ina R. *Flying Against the Wind: The Story of a Young Woman Who Defied the Nazis*. Brookline, MA: Lodgepole Press, 1995.

This well-written biography tells the little-known but compelling story of Cato Bjontes van Beek, a non-Jewish German executed at the age of 22 for writing and circulating anti-Nazi flyers. Before her arrest, Cato had also aided Jews in hiding, smuggled refugees over the Alps, and helped starving French prisoners of war. This biography is one of the few books on German resistance for younger readers.

Linnea, Sharon. *Raoul Wallenberg: The Man Who Stopped Death*. Philadelphia: Jewish Publication Society, 1993.

Linnea traces the life of the Swedish diplomat who saved Hungarian Jews during World War II and then mysteriously disappeared after the Soviet army occupied Budapest. This is an excellent, engaging biography for middle schoolers.

Marrin, Albert. *Hitler: A Portrait of a Tyrant*. New York: Viking, 1987.

Much more than a biography, Marrin provides a detailed look at both the man himself and the war he orchestrated. While he makes no effort to be objective in his portrayal of Hitler, the author gives the most detailed account of Hitler and Nazism available in books for young people.

Middle School (cont.)

Nicholson, Michael, and David Winner. *Raoul Wallenberg.* Ridgefield, CT: Morehouse, 1990.

This concise, well-illustrated biography contains considerable information about one of the best known of those individuals who helped rescue Jews during the Holocaust.

Pettit, Jane. *A Place to Hide: True Stories of Holocaust Rescues.* New York: Scholastic, 1993.

One of the most readable books for younger students, this collection includes the stories of Miep Gies, the Schindlers, and Denmark's rescue of its Jews.

Van der Rol, Ruud, and Rian Verhoeven. *Anne Frank Beyond the Diary: A Photographic Remembrance.* New York: Viking Press, 1993.

Compelling photographs from the Anne Frank House in Amsterdam and private collections provide a moving portrait of Anne Frank. Facts about Anne's life before and after her stay in the annex and the larger historical context constitute the text.

4. FICTION

Gehrts, Barbara. *Don't Say a Word.* New York: Macmillan, 1986.

Gehrts uses the novel form to describe her own experiences growing up in Nazi Germany as the daughter of an anti-Nazi Luftwaffe officer. Her work provides insight into historical events from an unusual perspective.

Laird, Christa. *Shadow of the Wall.* New York: Greenwillow, 1990.

Set in 1942 in the Warsaw ghetto, this novel features a boy living with his two younger sisters in Janusz Korczak's orphanage. This is short and much easier to read than Korczak's biography, and could either complement it or serve as an alternative to it.

Moskin, Marietta. *I Am Rosemarie.* New York: Dell Publishing Company, 1987.

A fictional composite of actual Dutch Jews, Rosemarie, like Anne Frank, was deported with her family to the Westerbork transit camp and eventually to Bergen-Belsen. Unlike Anne, however, Rosemarie and most of her family survive the harsh conditions described in this easy-to-read novel told in the first person.

Middle School
(cont.)

Orgel, Doris. *The Devil in Vienna.* **New York: Puffin, 1988.**

Based partly on the author's own experiences, this story is set in Vienna in the months leading up to the Nazi annexation of Austria in March 1938. Through her diary entries, a thirteen-year-old Jewish girl recounts the difficulties of maintaining her close friendship with the daughter of a Nazi.

Orlev, Uri. *The Man from the Other Side.* **Boston: Houghton Mifflin, 1991.**

This is the story of a non-Jewish boy living outside the Warsaw ghetto who joined his stepfather in smuggling goods into and people out of the ghetto. The author himself was a child in the ghetto and based his novel on the actual experiences of a childhood acquaintance.

Ramati, Alexander. *And the Violins Stopped Playing: A Story of the Gypsy Holocaust.* **New York: Franklin Watts, 1986.**

Written as a novel, this book is actually based on notes given to Ramati by Roman Mirga, a Polish Gypsy and the main character. It tells of Mirga's experiences from 1942 to 1945, when he escaped from Nazis in Poland only to be caught by them in Hungary and sent to Auschwitz.

Richter, Hans P. *Friedrich.* **New York: Puffin Books, 1987.**

Told in the first person, this autobiographical novel describes the friendship between two German boys, one Jewish and one not, and what happens to that relationship after the Nazis come to power and the non-Jewish boy's father joins the Nazi Party. The story is simple and easy to read, but a dramatic and powerful account, told from a child's perspective.

5. M**EMOIRS**

Auerbacher, Inge. *I Am a Star: Child of the Holocaust.* **New York: Prentice Hall, 1987.**

History, poetry, and personal narrative, accompanied by drawings and photographs, combine in this slim volume to present a concise, child's eye view of the Holocaust. From 1942 to 1945, Auerbacher was incarcerated in the Terezin ghetto in Czechoslovakia. This is an excellent personalized introduction to the Holocaust for younger readers.

Middle School
(cont.)

Drucker, Olga Levy. *Kindertransport*. New York: Holt, 1992.

Born in Germany in 1927, Olga Levy was one of the many Jewish children evacuated from Germany to England during 1938 and 1939. She was separated from her parents for six years, until they were reunited in the United States in 1945. She tells her story in a simple and moving way, adding historical facts of which she was unaware at the time, but which put her story into perspective. The book concludes with the reunion of former Kindertransport children in London in 1989.

Frank, Anne. *The Diary of a Young Girl*. New York: Pocket Books, c1953.

Still one of the most read works in Holocaust literature, this classic account presents an eloquent picture of adolescence for a Jewish girl growing up during the Holocaust years. The focus is more personal than historic, so accompanying background material is recommended to put it into historical perspective.

Isaacman, Clara, and Joan A. Grossman. *Clara's Story*. Philadelphia: Jewish Publication Society, 1984.

Originally from Romania, Clara and her family fled to Belgium in 1940. Like so many others, they were then threatened a second time by the Nazi invasion of Belgium. By constantly moving from one hiding place to another, everyone but Clara's father survived. Although her story parallels Anne Frank's in a number of ways, she adds more historical background to her personal narrative.

Koehn, Ilse. *Mischling, Second Degree: My Childhood in Nazi Germany*. New York: Puffin Books, 1990.

Unaware of her Jewish heritage, Ilse was six years old when the Nuremberg laws declared her a "Mischling, second degree," a person with one Jewish grandparent. Her story is simply that of a little girl whose comfortable world has been turned upside down for no apparent reason.

Leitner, Isabella. *The Big Lie: A True Story*. New York: Scholastic, 1992.

The author of *Fragments of Isabella,* one of the most eloquent memoirs written for adults, has successfully adapted her story for young readers. In spare, elegant prose, Leitner describes her deportation from Hungary in the summer of 1944, her experiences in Auschwitz, and her evacuation to Bergen-Belsen near the end of the war.

Middle School
(cont.)

Reiss, Johanna. *The Upstairs Room*. New York: HarperCollins, 1990.

From a Dutch Jewish family, Reiss tells the story of the years she spent hiding with her sister in the farmhouse of a Dutch family who protected them. She relates her experiences after the war in a sequel, *The Journey Back.*

Roth-Hano, Renee. *Touch Wood: A Girlhood in Occupied France*. New York: Puffin Books, 1989.

As a Jewish child in occupied France, the author and her two sisters found safe haven in a Catholic women's residence. Brought up "Catholic" to hide her true background, Roth-Hano discusses her confusion regarding her religious identity. She provides insight into her own situation and also that of many others who survived the Holocaust in a similar manner.

Sender, Ruth M. *The Cage*. New York: Macmillan, 1986.

Sender's account of her experiences is one of the most graphic and dramatic in young people's literature. Her story begins just before the Nazi invasion of Poland and continues through life in the Lodz ghetto and finally, at Auschwitz. A sequel, *To Life,* continues her narrative from liberation to her arrival in the United States in 1950.

Toll, Nelly S. *Behind the Secret Window: A Memoir of a Hidden Childhood*. New York: Dial Books, 1993.

Toll recounts the details of her family life in Lwów, Poland, before World War II and her experiences, told from a child's perspective, of her eighteen months in hiding with her mother. The readable narrative is accompanied by twenty-nine reproductions of Toll's colorful and poignant watercolor paintings that she created during those difficult months.

Wiesel, Elie. *Night*. New York: Bantam, 1982.

Wiesel is one of the most eloquent writers of the Holocaust, and this book is his best-known work. This compelling narrative describes his own experience in Auschwitz. His account of his entrance into Auschwitz and his first night in the camp is extraordinary. This narrative is often considered required reading for students of the Holocaust.

Middle School (cont.)

Wolff, Marion Freyer. *The Shrinking Circle: Memories of Nazi Berlin*. New York: UAHC Press, 1989.

This poignant, sensitive memoir of the author's childhood in Nazi Berlin sets her personal history in the larger context of political changes and anti-Jewish policies in Berlin of the 1930s.

Zar, Rose. *In the Mouth of the Wolf*. Philadelphia: Jewish Publication Society, 1983.

Zar's story is unusual because she is one of the few Polish Jews who survived the Holocaust years in Poland without going into hiding. With false papers, she was able to secure a job working in the household of an SS officer and his wife.

6. ART

Bernbaum, Israel. *My Brother's Keeper: The Holocaust Through the Eyes of an Artist*. New York: Putnam, 1985.

This book is based on a series of five paintings called "Warsaw Ghetto 1943," which the author created to portray people and events inside and on the periphery of the ghetto. Bernbaum himself escaped from Warsaw shortly before the ghetto was established. While many of the details in these paintings are lost in the small reproductions, the artist's explanation of his symbols and images makes them more accessible to young people.

Innocenti, Roberto. *Rose Blanche*. New York: Stewart Tabori & Chang, 1991.

This appears to be a picture book intended for very young children. On another level, it is an artistic expression of the Holocaust as seen through the eyes of a child; it conveys the child's failure to understand or accept the events that take place around her.

Volavkova, Hana, ed. *I Never Saw Another Butterfly: Children's Drawings and Poems from Terezin Concentration Camp 1942–1944*. New York: Schocken, 1993.

A poignant memorial to the children of Terezin, the collages, paintings, drawings, and poems published in this selection are impressive for their artistic merit and their value in documenting the feelings and lives of children in the camp. Some prior knowledge of what life in the camps was like will make these pieces more meaningful to students.

High School   **1. HISTORY, GENERAL**

Bauer, Yehuda, and Nili Keren. *A History of the Holocaust.* New York: Franklin Watts, 1982.

Broader in scope than the title indicates, this work examines the origins of antisemitism and Nazism as well as the history of Jewish-German relationships. Bauer also arranges material on the Holocaust by individual country; this is useful for following events as they affected each occupied nation and for demonstrating the scope of the Holocaust. One of the most readable general histories for high school students.

Gilbert, Martin. *The Holocaust: A History of the Jews in Europe during the Second World War.* New York: Henry Holt and Company, 1986.

Gilbert combines historical narrative with personal testimonies of survivors. Although the book is long, excerpts can easily be handled by students. It is also well-indexed, making it an invaluable tool for providing supplementary material on almost any aspect of the Holocaust.

Hilberg, Raul. *The Destruction of the European Jews* [student text]. New York: Holmes and Meier, 1985.

This edition of Hilberg's classic work is an abridgement of the original, three-volume edition. The focus here is on the Nazis and their destruction process, from the concentration of the Jews in ghettos to the killing operations of the mobile units and the death camps. This essential history is recommended for more advanced students.

Hilberg, Raul. *Perpetrators, Victims, Bystanders: The Jewish Catastrophe, 1933–1945.* New York: HarperCollins, 1992.

In his most recent work, Hilberg expands his focus from the study of the perpetrator alone to include, as the title indicates, victims and bystanders. He also includes rescuers and Jewish resisters, groups which he ignored in his earlier work; however, the attention he gives to these groups is minimal. His main focus continues to be on the destruction and those responsible for it. Hitler's role is more central here than in the earlier work. This is Hilberg's most accessible book.

Yahil, Leni. *The Holocaust: The Fate of European Jewry, 1932–1945.* **New York: Oxford, 1991.**

The chronological approach used here groups the material into three broad time periods: 1932–39, 1939–41, and 1941–45. About two-thirds of the book deals with the period 1941–45, with major emphasis on the "Final Solution." This is a valuable research tool for advanced students, and excerpts on specific topics can be used more generally.

2. HISTORY, SPECIALIZED

Abzug, Robert H. *Inside the Vicious Heart: Americans and the Liberation of Nazi Concentration Camps.* **New York: Oxford University Press, 1985.**

Using the diaries, letters, photographs, and oral testimonies of American GIs and journalists, Abzug analyzes the reactions of the first eyewitnesses who entered the liberated concentration camps in Germany and Austria during the spring of 1945. This highly readable account is liberally illustrated with photographs.

Adelson, Alan, and Robert Lapides, eds. *Lodz Ghetto: Inside a Community Under Siege.* **New York: Viking Penguin, 1991.**

As the source book for the Lodz ghetto film, this work is an excellent supplement to the documentary, but it also stands on its own. It contains both German and ghetto documents as well as the personal expressions of ghetto residents in a variety of forms, including diaries, speeches, paintings, photographs, essays, and poems.

Allen, William S. *The Nazi Seizure of Power: The Experience of a Single German Town, 1922–1945.* **Revised edition. New York: Franklin Watts, 1984.**

Northeim, a small town of medieval origins in the center of prewar Germany, is the setting for this absorbing study of the impact of Nazism on a single community. As one of the few detailed local studies of Nazi Germany available in English, this book is an invaluable complement to histories of Nazism from the national perspective.

Arad, Yitzhak. *Ghetto in Flames.* **New York: Holocaust Publications, 1982.**

For centuries, its large number of rabbinic scholars assured Vilna a central place in the cultural life of Lithuanian Jewry. Arad's scholarly and groundbreaking study focuses upon the life, struggle, and annihilation of the Jews of Vilna in the period between 1941 and 1944.

High School
(cont.)

Block, Gay, and Malka Drucker. *Rescuers: Portraits of Moral Courage in the Holocaust.* New York: Holmes and Meier, 1992.

The interviews and full-size color portraits are of 49 ordinary individuals from 10 countries who risked their lives to help Jews by hiding them, sharing their food rations, forging passports and baptismal certificates, and raising Jewish children as their own. The rescuers' portraits are presented by country of origin, and a brief historical overview of rescue efforts in each country precedes their personal stories.

Conot, Robert E. *Justice at Nuremberg.* New York: Carroll & Graf, 1984.

In addition to the detailed history of the Nuremberg Trials, Conot discusses the preparations for the trials. He also goes beyond the events of the trials themselves to discuss the difficulties involved in creating and implementing an international legal entity.

Des Pres, Terrence. *The Survivor: An Anatomy of Life in the Death Camps.* New York: Oxford University Press, 1976.

Des Pres studies survivors of the death camps in an attempt to determine what enabled people to survive; his conclusions are controversial and are unlike those of Bettelheim (*The Informed Heart*), Frankl (*Man's Search for Meaning*), and other Holocaust survivors.

Flender, Harold. *Rescue in Denmark.* New York: Anti-Defamation League, 1963.

The exceptional, honorable character of the Danes' successful operation to rescue most of its Jewish residents has aroused profound admiration. Individual stories of rescue are cited here, as well as more general historical background and a look at the reasons for the Nazis' failure to implement the "Final Solution" in Denmark.

Friedman, Philip. *Their Brothers' Keepers: The Christian Heroes and Heroines Who Helped the Oppressed Escape the Nazi Terror.* New York: Anti-Defamation League, 1978.

One of the first studies of Christians who rescued Jews during the Holocaust, this work was originally published in 1957. It is primarily an overview of rescue activities, although some stories of individual rescue are told. Background material and activities for individual countries are included.

High School   **Josephs, Jeremy. *Swastika Over Paris: The Fate of the Jews in France*. New**
(cont.)   **York: Arcade Publishing, 1989.**

In this highly readable work, Josephs tells the story of French Jews during the Holocaust by focusing on two Jews of widely different class backgrounds. One was the only member of the well-known Rothschild family to remain in France during the German occupation; the other was the 16-year-old daughter of working-class parents and a member of the French Resistance.

Mayer, Milton. *They Thought They Were Free: The Germans 1933–45*. Chicago: University of Chicago Press, 1966.

After the war, Mayer, an American journalist, interviewed ten men of different backgrounds but from the same German town in an effort to determine, through their eyes, what had happened in Germany and what had made it possible. This is an excellent companion to Allen's *Nazi Seizure of Power*.

Patterson, Charles. *Anti-Semitism: The Road to the Holocaust and Beyond*. New York: Walker and Company, 1988.

As the title implies, this history of antisemitism includes the years both before and after the Holocaust. Patterson begins with ancient and medieval times and concludes with a discussion of modern antisemitism in various parts of the world.

Plant, Richard. *The Pink Triangle: The Nazi War against Homosexuals*. New York: Henry Holt, 1986.

The Nazis condemned homosexuals as "socially aberrant." Soon after Hitler came to power in 1933, Storm Troopers raided nightclubs and other places where homosexuals met. About 10,000 people were imprisoned as homosexuals, and many of them perished in concentration camps. In the camps, homosexuals' uniforms sometimes bore a pink triangular badge as an identifying mark. In this volume, the first comprehensive study available in English, Plant examines the ideological motivations for the Nazi persecution of homosexuals and the history of the implementation of Nazi policies.

High School
(cont.)

Read, Anthony, and David Fisher. *Kristallnacht: The Tragedy of the Nazi Night of Terror.* **New York: Random House, 1989.**

Beginning with a brief background and ending with the Evian conference, the focus of this work is the events of *Kristallnacht* itself and its immediate aftermath, including the German response, the Nazi follow-up, and the international response. Both the prologue and epilogue deal with Herschel Grynszpan, the young man who triggered *Kristallnacht* by shooting a German officer in Paris.

Rittner, Carol, and Sondra Meyers, eds. *The Courage to Care: Rescuers of Jews during the Holocaust.* **New York: New York University Press, 1989.**

Taken from the film of the same name, the book presents vignettes from rescuers and those rescued in a variety of countries, with additional commentaries from historians and writers. This is a particularly valuable resource when used with the film.

Szner, Zvi, and Alexander Sened, eds. *With a Camera in the Ghetto.* **New York: Schocken, 1987.**

Mendel Grossman was the only Jewish photographer who succeeded in capturing a ghetto on film; his pictures depict life in the Lodz ghetto in 1941 and 1942. This is an excellent companion to the Lodz ghetto film and the Adelson book. It can also supplement the book if the film is not available.

3. Biography

Bierman, John. *Righteous Gentile: The Story of Raoul Wallenberg, Missing Hero of the Holocaust.* **New York: Anti-Defamation League, 1981.**

Only the first half of the book is truly a biography of this well-known figure who helped save at least 30,000 Jews in Hungary. The second part of the book describes the circumstances surrounding Wallenberg's disappearance and subsequent attempts to locate him or at least find out what happened to him.

Breitman, Richard, and Walter Laqueur. *Breaking the Silence: The Man Who Exposed the Final Solution.* **Hanover, NH: University Press of New England, 1986.**

Eduard Schulte was a major German industrialist who abhorred Hitler and Nazism. He is the man credited with passing on to the Allies news not only of troop movements and weapon programs but of the Nazi plans for genocide. This biography relates Schulte's story from his childhood to his postwar years. The authors also describe the responses of Allied governments to the information he passed on to them.

High School
(cont.)   **Lifton, Betty Jean. *The King of Children: A Portrait of Janusz Korczak.* New York: Schocken, 1989.**

Much of the material in this biography is taken from Korczak's diaries, but Lifton also interviewed many of his former charges and people who worked with him. In addition to the personal portrait of Korczak, she includes background material on the Warsaw ghetto based on Korczak's diary and diaries of other ghetto victims.

Scholl, Inge. *The White Rose: Munich, 1942–43.* Middletown, CT: Wesleyan, 1983.

Inge Scholl was the sister of Hans and Sophie Scholl, founders of the famous "White Rose" resistance movement in Germany. Originally written in 1952, this is the story of the Scholls and of the White Rose movement. It also includes original documents concerning their indictments and sentences. This book was previously published under the title *Students against Tyranny.*

Spiegelman, Art. *Maus* [vols. I & II]. New York: Pantheon, 1991.

Spiegelman uses his talents as a cartoonist to present his parents' experiences during the Holocaust in a unique way; here cartoon characters represent people, with the Jews portrayed as mice and the Nazis as cats. In the first volume, the author relates the real-life trials of his parents at Auschwitz. The second volume continues their story from Auschwitz to America. The cartoon format will appeal to reluctant readers, and the satirical irony of these works make them appropriate for a wide audience.

4. FICTION

Appelfeld, Aharon. *To the Land of the Cattails.* New York: Weidenfeld and Nicolson, 1986.

A young man and his mother living in Austria travel eastward across the heart of Europe to the distant land of her childhood. The year is 1938 and the two arrive just as the Jews of the village are being shipped off on a mysterious train to an unspecified destination. Appelfeld is a master storyteller, and this haunting narrative of an ironic pilgrimage will not easily be forgotten.

Fink, Ida. *A Scrap of Time.* New York: Schocken, 1989.

The title story in this collection of short stories concerns the way time was measured by Holocaust victims. Other stories describe people in a variety of normal human situations distorted by the circumstances of the times. Many of these stories can be effectively used with students.

High School (cont.)

Friedlander, Albert. *Out of the Whirlwind.* **New York: Schocken, 1989.**

Not all of the entries included in this anthology are fiction. Excerpts are also included from historical works and personal narratives. The book is arranged thematically, making it especially helpful for a teacher looking for material to support specific aspects of a curriculum.

Glatstein, Jacob. *Anthology of Holocaust Literature.* **New York: Macmillan, 1973.**

Chapters in this collection cover life in the ghettos, children, the camps, resistance, and non-Jewish victims. Excerpts are included from both works of fiction and primary source materials such as diaries, memoirs, and ghetto documents. Many of these pieces can be especially useful if teachers provide additional background information on the authors and context of the writings.

Lustig, Arnold. *Darkness Casts No Shadows.* **Evanston, IL: Northwestern University Press, 1985.**

Two young boys escape from a transport between a concentration camp and an unknown destination that would probably turn out to be a killing center. They are also trying to escape from the memories of their past experiences and are searching for a home that no longer exists. Far from the typical romanticized escape novel, this is a sensitive but unsentimental look at the child in war.

Ozick, Cynthia. *The Shawl.* **New York: Random House, 1990.**

Originally published as two separate stories in *The New Yorker,* the title story tells of a mother witnessing her baby's death at the hands of camp guards. Another story, "Rose," describes that same mother 30 years later, still haunted by that event. This is Holocaust fiction at its best, brief but unforgettable.

Ramati, Alexander. *And the Violins Stopped Playing: A Story of the Gypsy Holocaust.* **New York: Franklin Watts, 1986.**

Written as a novel, this book is actually based on notes given to Ramati by Roman Mirga, a Polish Gypsy and the main character. It tells of Mirga's experiences from 1942 to 1945, when he escaped from Nazis in Poland only to be caught by them in Hungary and sent to Auschwitz.

High School
(cont.)

Uhlman, Fred. *Reunion*. New York: Farrar, Straus & Giroux, 1977.

More a novella than a novel, this brief but moving story told in retrospect by a Jewish-German youth describes his friendship with a non-Jewish German youth during the 1930s. Its brevity and readability make it especially suitable for reluctant readers.

5. MEMOIRS

Eliach, Yaffa. *Hasidic Tales of the Holocaust*. New York: Vintage Books, 1988.

Through interviews and oral histories, Eliach garnered eighty-nine tales, both true stories and fanciful legends. This beautiful, compelling collection bears witness, in a traditional idiom, to the victims' suffering, dying, and surviving.

Gies, Miep, and Alison L. Gold. *Anne Frank Remembered: The Story of the Woman Who Helped to Hide the Frank Family*. New York: Simon & Schuster, 1988.

Miep Gies, along with her husband, were among the people who helped the Frank family while they were in hiding. Her story is an important supplement to Anne Frank's diary as it adds historical background as well as an outside perspective to Anne's story. Gies enables the reader to understand what was happening both inside and outside the Annex.

Gurdus, Luba K. *The Death Train*. New York: Holocaust Publications, 1987.

The title encapsulates the author's story of her Holocaust experiences. She and her family spent a considerable amount of time either on a transport or in a hideout near the train tracks in their desperate, and ultimately unsuccessful, attempt to avoid the camps. She illustrates her memoir with original drawings, which give an additional personal touch to what is already a very personal and moving account.

Leitner, Isabella. *Fragments of Isabella: A Memoir of Auschwitz*. New York: Dell, 1983.

A survivor of Auschwitz recounts the ordeal of holding her family together after their mother is killed in the camp. This slim volume is an eloquent account of survival in the midst of chaos and destruction. A glossary of death camp language is a valuable addition. Leitner's story is continued in *Saving the Fragments*.

Levi, Primo. *Survival in Auschwitz.* **New York: Macmillan, 1987.**

Levi was an Italian Jew captured in 1943 and still at Auschwitz at the time of the liberation. He not only chronicles the daily activities in the camp, but his inner reactions to it and the destruction of the inner as well as the outer self. This memoir is one of the most important books on the Holocaust.

Meed, Vladka. *On Both Sides of the Wall.* **New York: Holocaust Publications, 1979.**

This is an informative memoir of the Warsaw ghetto by one of the young smugglers who maintained contact between the ghetto and the Aryan side of the city. Working for the Jewish Combat Organization (ZOB), Vladka Meed helped smuggle weapons and ammunition into the ghetto.

Nir, Yehuda. *The Lost Childhood.* **San Diego: Harcourt Brace Jovanovich, 1991.**

This compelling memoir chronicles six extraordinary years in the life of a Polish Jewish boy, his mother, and his sister, who all survived the Holocaust by obtaining false papers and posing as Catholics. Yehuda Nir lost almost everything, including his father, his possessions, his youth and innocence, and his identity, but he managed to live with the help of chance, personal resourcefulness, and the support of his family.

Senesh, Hannah. *Hannah Senesh: Her Life and Diary.* **New York: Schocken Books, 1972.**

A native of Hungary, Senesh moved to Palestine just before World War II and later joined a parachute corps formed by the British. She was captured and later executed after her final mission, to warn Hungarian Jews about the "Final Solution." This volume includes the diary Senesh kept from the age of thirteen, many of her poems and letters, and memoirs by her mother and others who knew her.

Tec, Nechama. *Dry Tears: The Story of a Lost Childhood.* **New York: Oxford University Press, 1984.**

The author and her family were Polish Jews who survived the Holocaust on the Aryan side of the ghetto. Although she escaped the worst horrors of the Holocaust, her story adds another dimension to Holocaust literature. She describes her childhood experiences as seen through the child's eyes, but with the added retrospective of her adult perception.

High School
(cont.)

Wiesel, Elie. *Night*. New York: Bantam, 1982.

Wiesel is one of the most eloquent writers of the Holocaust, and this book is his best-known work. This compelling narrative describes his own experience in Auschwitz. His account of his entrance into Auschwitz and his first night in the camp is extraordinary. This narrative is often considered required reading for students of the Holocaust.

Yoors, Jan. *Crossing: A Journal of Survival and Resistance in World War II*. New York: Simon and Schuster, 1971.

Every summer during his teen years, Yoors left his comfortable, upper-middle-class family life in Belgium to travel around Europe with a Rom (Gypsy) family. This beautifully written journal focuses on the participation of Yoors and his fondly remembered Rom friends in resistance activities during World War II.

6. ART

Volavkova, Hana, ed. *I Never Saw Another Butterfly: Children's Drawings and Poems from Terezin Concentration Camp 1942–1944*. New York: Schocken, 1993.

A poignant memorial to the children of Terezin, the collages, drawings, and poems published in this selection are impressive for their artistic merit and their value in documenting the feelings and lives of the children in the camp. Some prior knowledge of what life in the camp was like will make this book more meaningful to students.

Adult

1. GENERAL HISTORY

Berenbaum, Michael. *The World Must Know: A History of the Holocaust as Told in the United States Holocaust Memorial Museum*. Boston: Little Brown, 1993.

As indicated by the title, the book tells the story of the Holocaust as presented in the museum. It includes over 200 photos from the museum's archives and artifact collection and many eyewitness accounts from the museum's oral and video history collections. The three parts of the book, which correspond to the three main exhibition floors, cover the rise of the Nazis to power; the ghettos and camps; and rescue, resistance, and the postwar period.

Adult
(cont.)

Dawidowicz, Lucy. *The War Against the Jews 1933–1945.* New York: Bantam, 1986.

Dawidowicz raises three questions: How was it possible for a modern state to carry out the systematic murder of a people for no reason other than that they were Jewish? How did European Jewry allow itself to be destroyed? How could the world stand by without halting this destruction? In Dawidowicz's view, World War II was the direct result of Hitler's antisemitism; she believes the war was waged to allow the Nazis to implement the "Final Solution."

Dawidowicz, Lucy. *A Holocaust Reader.* West Orange, NJ: Behrman House, 1976.

A companion to the historical work cited above, here Dawidowicz presents documentation to support the history. Both German and Jewish documents are provided, including reports, letters, and diaries. The general introduction to studying Holocaust documents and the introductions to each section of documents are extremely helpful.

Gilbert, Martin. *The Holocaust: A History of the Jews in Europe during the Second World War.* New York: Henry Holt and Company, 1986.

Gilbert effectively combines the results of historical research with personal narratives of survivors. Although the book is long, it is readable and extremely well-indexed, making it an invaluable tool for providing supplementary material on almost any aspect of the Holocaust.

Hayes, Peter, ed. *Lessons and Legacies: The Meaning of the Holocaust in a Changing World.* Evanston, IL: Northwestern University Press, 1991.

In this useful collection thoughtfully introduced by Hayes, various aspects of the Holocaust are examined by sixteen leading scholars including Raul Hilberg, Saul Friedländer, Yehuda Bauer, Michael Marrus, Christopher Browning, and Lawrence Langer. Also included is a critical essay by Alvin Rosenfeld on the popularization of Anne Frank.

Hilberg, Raul. *The Destruction of the European Jews* [3 vols.]. New York: Holmes and Meier, 1985.

This authoritative reconstruction of the Holocaust remains the standard text to which all others are compared. Hilberg's primary focus is on the methods of the Nazi murder process, including the organizational and bureaucratic machinery of destruction. Hilberg's explanation of the role of Jews themselves in their destruction and of the lack of resistance has been criticized.

Adult
(cont.)

Hilberg, Raul. *Perpetrators, Victims, Bystanders: The Jewish Catastrophe, 1933–1945.* New York: HarperCollins, 1992.

In his most recent work, Hilberg expands his focus from the study of the perpetrator alone to include, as the title indicates, victims and bystanders. He also includes rescuers and Jewish resisters, groups which he ignored in his earlier work; however, the attention he gives to these groups is minimal. His main focus continues to be on the destruction and those responsible for it. Hitler's role is more central here than in the earlier work. This is Hilberg's most accessible book.

Levin, Nora. *The Holocaust: The Nazi Destruction of European Jewry, 1933–1945.* Melbourne, FL: Krieger Publishing Company, 1990.

Levin was one of the first writers to use the term Holocaust for the destruction of the Jews of Europe during World War II. The first part of this historical account, arranged chronologically, details the Nazi plan and implementation of the "Final Solution." The second half, arranged geographically, shows how the Nazi program was affected by individual governments and by degrees of antisemitism. Levin emphasizes the resistance of the Jews and rejects the notion that they went to their deaths "like sheep to the slaughter."

Yahil, Leni. *The Holocaust: The Fate of European Jewry, 1932–1945.* New York: Oxford, 1991.

This is one of the most comprehensive histories of the Holocaust. Yahil demonstrates how the Nazis used the anti-Jewish program from the beginning to reinforce their power. Before the war, their deliberate violence against the Jews of Germany helped to terrorize the rest of the country, and during the war, their anti-Jewish policies were used as an excuse for taking control of the governments of satellites and occupied countries.

2. History, Specialized

Allen, William S. *The Nazi Seizure of Power: The Experience of a Single German Town, 1922–1945.* Revised edition. New York: Franklin Watts, 1984.

Northeim, a small town of medieval origins in the center of prewar Germany, is the setting for this absorbing study of the impact of Nazism on a single community. As one of the only detailed local studies of Nazi Germany available in English, this book is an invaluable complement to histories of Nazism from the national perspective.

Adult
(cont.)

Bartoszewski, Wladyslaw T. *The Warsaw Ghetto: A Christian's Testimony.* Boston: Beacon Press, 1988.

The author is a Polish historian and journalist, born in Warsaw in 1922, now a retired professor of Catholic University in Lublin. He returned to Warsaw from Auschwitz in 1941 and served as liaison between the Polish underground and Jewish ghetto leadership. In this work he intermingles his personal story with primary source material from Nazi, resistance, and ghetto documents.

Bauer, Yehuda, and Nathan Rotenstreich, eds. *The Holocaust as Historical Experience.* New York: Holmes and Meier, 1981.

This collection of essays was specifically designed for teachers. It is divided into three sections, dealing with background, case studies and witnesses, and responses by Jews. The essays cover a variety of ways of approaching the Holocaust, and the work helps to set a framework for historical research.

Berenbaum, Michael, ed. *A Mosaic of Victims: Non-Jews Persecuted and Murdered by the Nazis.* New York: New York University Press, 1990.

This collection of essays includes entries by a number of noted Holocaust scholars, including Berenbaum himself. The subjects of the essays include non-Jewish victims such as homosexuals, Gypsies, Serbs, Slavs, and pacifists.

Bridenthal, Renate, et al. *When Biology Became Destiny: Women in Weimar and Nazi Germany.* New York: Monthly Review Press, 1984.

Claudia Koonz and Sybil Milton are among the authors included in this collection of essays dealing with a variety of topics and issues relating to women and families in Germany in the 1920s, 1930s, and 1940s. Politics, feminism, and anti-semitism are among the subjects addressed.

Browning, Christopher. *Ordinary Men: Reserve Battalion 101 and the Final Solution in Poland.* New York: HarperCollins, 1992.

In this compelling, pioneering social history, Browning attempts to explain how "ordinary," middle-aged men became mass murderers, personally shooting thousands of men, women, and children in occupied Poland where the reservists served as members of the German Order Police. The author draws on the judicial interrogations of 210 men who provided testimony in the 1960s regarding their participation in the massacres and roundups of Jews in 1942 and 1943.

*Adult
(cont.)*

Burleigh, Michael, and Wolfgang Wipperman. *The Racial State: Germany 1933–1945.* **New York: Cambridge University Press, 1991.**

Between 1933 and 1945 the Nazi regime tried to restructure German society along racial lines. This important, scholarly study shows how the Nazis' plan to annihilate European Jewry derived from racial and population policies that also targeted the Sinti and Roma (Gypsies), the mentally and physically handicapped, the "asocial," and homosexuals.

Conot, Robert E. *Justice at Nuremberg.* **New York: Carroll & Graf, 1984.**

In addition to the detailed history of the Nuremberg Trials, Conot discusses the preparations for the trials. He also goes beyond the events of the trials themselves to discuss the difficulties involved in creating and implementing an international legal entity.

Des Pres, Terrence. *The Survivor: An Anatomy of Life in the Death Camps.* **New York: Oxford University Press, 1976.**

Des Pres studies survivors of the death camps in an attempt to determine what enabled people to survive. His conclusions are controversial and are unlike those of Bettelheim (*The Informed Heart*), Frankl (*Man's Search for Meaning*), and other Holocaust scholars.

Dobroszycki, Lucjan, ed. *The Chronicle of the Lodz Ghetto.* **New Haven, CT: Yale University Press, 1987.**

Himself a survivor of the Lodz ghetto, Dobroszycki introduces and analyzes the detailed records kept by Lodz archivists. He includes material about the ghetto's controversial leader, Mordecai Chaim Rumkowski.

Dwork, Debórah. *Children with a Star: Jewish Youth in Nazi Europe.* **New Haven, CT: Yale University Press, 1991.**

This detailed study of Jewish children during the Holocaust is based on archival material and survivor interviews. Focusing on the daily life of children, the book includes a variety of experiences: children at home, in hiding, and in transit camps, ghettos, forced labor camps, and killing centers.

Adult
(cont.)

Engelman, Bernt. *In Hitler's Germany.* **New York: Schocken, 1988.**

Engelman, a German raised in an anti-Nazi home, tells his own story here along with those of other Germans both for and against the Nazis. He also includes those who resisted and those who were indifferent to or unaware of the events around them. This is a social history, focusing on everyday life.

Epstein, Helen. *Children of the Holocaust.* **New York: Viking Penguin, 1988.**

Epstein, who is a daughter of survivors, interviewed many other children of survivors and presents here a wide range of their responses. She integrates her own story into the text and deals with the issues raised by both parents and children.

Evans, Richard. *In Hitler's Shadow: West German Historians and the Attempt to Escape from the Nazi Past.* **New York: Pantheon, 1989.**

This noted British historian examines the work of West German historians and the controversial attempts to diminish Germany's responsibility for the Holocaust. Some of their arguments resemble those used by the Nazis themselves. Evans distinguishes between individual and collective guilt, and discusses President Ronald Reagan and the Bitburg Cemetery visit.

Fein, Helen. *Accounting for Genocide: National Responses and Jewish Victimization during the Holocaust.* **Chicago: University of Chicago Press, 1984.**

After examining the nature and causes of genocide and the history of anti-semitism, Fein addresses the varying patterns of genocide in countries during the Holocaust and the way those differences were influenced by each nation's history and culture. After looking at these events from the broad historical perspective, she takes a second look from the perspective of the victim.

Feingold, Henry. *The Politics of Rescue: The Roosevelt Administration and the Holocaust, 1938–1945.* **New York: Schocken, 1980.**

This evenhanded, scholarly study examines the reaction of the Roosevelt Administration to the Holocaust. Feingold attempts to move beyond a moral condemnation of American inaction to examine the political context that shaped the American response. The main focus is on American and international refugee policy from the Evian Conference in 1938 to the creation of the War Refugee Board in 1944.

Adult
(cont.)

Gallagher, Hugh Gregory. *By Trust Betrayed: Patients, Physicians, and the License to Kill in the Third Reich.* Arlington, VA: Vandemeer Press, 1995.

A paraplegic, Gallagher has provided a compelling account of Nazi Germany's so-called "euthanasia" program that enabled German physicians to kill mentally and physically handicapped persons deemed "unworthy of life."

Gellately, Robert. *The Gestapo and German Society: Enforcing Racial Policy.* New York: Oxford University Press, 1992.

In this original, scholarly study of the Nazi secret police, Gellately combines administrative and social history. He draws extensively on Gestapo case files to show that the key factor in the enforcement of Nazi racial policy designed to isolate Jews was the willingness of German citizens to provide the authorities with information about suspected "criminality." The author includes a chapter on racial policy aimed at Polish foreign workers.

Gutman, Yisrael, and Michael Berenbaum, eds. *Anatomy of the Auschwitz Death Camp.* Bloomington: Indiana University Press, 1994.

Twenty-nine essays by scholars on all aspects of Auschwitz, including its construction, operations, perpetrators, and victims, comprise this comprehensive volume published in association with the United States Holocaust Memorial Museum.

Herzstein, Robert E. *Roosevelt and Hitler: Prelude to War.* New York: John Wiley & Sons, 1994.

This book is important as it provides the larger political context in which American responses to the Holocaust took place. Herzstein argues that President Roosevelt was an early, decisive, and masterful opponent of Hitler who foresaw the true extent of the Nazi threat both at home and abroad. The author documents pro-Nazi activities in prewar United States that were supported by the German government and Roosevelt's success in discrediting American far-right and antisemitic movements between 1938 and 1941.

Herzstein, Robert E. *The War that Hitler Won: Goebbels and the Nazi Media Campaign.* New York: Paragon House, 1978.

The author illustrates the power of propaganda and the effective manipulation of mass media by focusing on the work of Goebbels and the effect of that work on the German people.

Adult
(cont.)

Horwitz, Gordon. *In the Shadow of Death: Living Outside the Gates of Mauthausen*. New York: The Free Press, 1990.

How much did people living near the camps know about what was going on? How did they cope with this knowledge? How did they find out? These and similar questions are raised in this very readable book on the complicity of bystanders in the Holocaust.

Kamenetsky, Christa. *Children's Literature in Hitler's Germany: The Cultural Policy of National Socialism*. Athens, OH: Ohio University Press, 1986.

Not only was new literature created to support the Nazi philosophy, but old literature, including traditional folklore, was adapted to reflect Nazi principles. Kamenetsky discusses this aspect of the Nazi attempt to control what children read, and also looks at censorship, school reform, and control of libraries and publishers.

Klee, Ernst, et al., eds. *The Good Old Days: The Holocaust as Seen by Its Perpetrators and Bystanders*. New York: Free Press, 1991.

Originally published in Germany in 1988, this work is made up of letters, diaries, reports, photographs, and other documents, some of which were kept in scrapbooks and albums by people like concentration camp guards, SS officers, and other perpetrators and "sympathetic observers" of the Holocaust.

Koonz, Claudia. *Mothers in the Fatherland: Women, the Family and Nazi Politics*. New York: St. Martin's Press, 1988.

A history of the women's movement in Germany from the Weimar Republic to the Nazi era, this work emphasizes the role of women in Nazi Germany and the impact of Nazism on the family unit. Koonz also includes material on the influence of the church in defining women's roles, on female members of the resistance, and on Jewish women.

Langer, Lawrence L. *Holocaust Testimonies: The Ruins of Memory*. New Haven, CT: Yale University Press, 1991.

After looking at hundreds of video interviews with Holocaust survivors, Langer notes the characteristics that distinguish oral testimony from the more traditional written form. These distinctions influence both the survivor and the viewer of video testimonies; they also provide a different perspective on survival theories.

Adult
(cont.)

Lanzmann, Claude. *Shoah: An Oral History of the Holocaust.* New York: Pantheon, 1987.

This work consists of the text of Lanzmann's nine-and-a-half hour film of the same name. The film's length makes the text extremely useful to the teacher, facilitating the process of selecting excerpts for classroom use. The text can also be used alone if the film is unavailable.

Laska, Vera. *Women in the Resistance and in the Holocaust: The Voices of Eyewitnesses.* Westport, CT: Greenwood Publishing Group, 1983.

Laska has collected more than two dozen accounts of women during the Holocaust, stressing women's resistance activities. The material is divided into three sections: resistance, hiding, and the camps. These are all first-person accounts, many of them excerpts from diaries and memoirs, and they represent a number of different countries.

Lifton, Robert. *The Nazi Doctors: Medical Killings and the Psychology of Genocide.* New York: Basic Books, 1988.

Based on German records as well as on interviews with Nazi doctors, prison doctors, and survivors of the camps, Lifton not only documents the role doctors played but also suggests ways they were able to rationalize their role.

Lipstadt, Deborah. *Beyond Belief: The American Press & the Coming of the Holocaust 1933–1945.* New York: The Free Press, 1986.

Why did one of every three Americans polled in 1943 dismiss as propaganda reports of atrocities against European Jews? Why were reports given by Auschwitz escapees in 1944 viewed with skepticism by major newspapers? Lipstadt raises these questions and others in this book on how the American news media reported (or ignored) the Nazi persecution and genocide of European Jewry.

Lipstadt, Deborah. *Denying the Holocaust: The Growing Assault on Truth and Memory.* New York: The Free Press, 1993.

Lipstadt does not refute the deniers of the Holocaust point by point (although she offers a useful appendix addressing some of their specific charges). Instead she provides an overview of the main figures promoting denial in the U.S. and abroad, their motives, their methods, and an assessment of their impact on college campuses and wider public opinion.

Adult
(cont.)
Lukas, Richard C. *The Forgotten Holocaust: The Poles under German Occupation, 1939–1944.* Lexington: The University Press of Kentucky, 1986.

The Nazis viewed Poles as subhumans occupying lands vital to Germany. After Germany conquered Poland in 1939, the Nazis expelled Poles from whole regions and resettled the land with Germans. Many Polish civilians were murdered, including thousands of priests, teachers, writers, and other intellectual and political leaders. Lukas documents the Polish suffering through interviews, Polish archival material, and published sources.

Mandell, Richard. *The Nazi Olympics.* Champaign, IL: University of Illinois Press, 1988.

The 1936 Olympics became a political event as much as an athletic one. Mandell chronicles both aspects and discusses the importance of the Nazi use of pageantry.

Marrus, Michael. *The Holocaust in History.* New York: New American Library/Dutton, 1989.

In this intelligent and succinct evaluation of historical accounts of the Holocaust, Marrus looks at a variety of issues: antisemitism, collaboration, resistance, and others. He presents the interpretations of leading historians in these areas and points out the strengths and weaknesses of their arguments. At no time does he allow this to become an intellectual exercise; instead, he is searching for better understanding.

Mayer, Milton. *They Thought They Were Free: The Germans 1933–45.* Chicago: University of Chicago Press, 1966.

After the war, this American journalist interviewed ten men of different backgrounds from the same German town in an effort to determine through their eyes what had happened in Germany and what had made it possible. This is an excellent companion to Allen's *Nazi Seizure of Power.*

Morse, Arthur D. *While Six Million Died: A Chronicle of American Apathy.* New York: Overlook Press, 1985.

The term "American apathy" that Morse uses in his title refers less to the American public than to the United States government. Using primary source materials, Morse details the process by which the government responded, or failed to respond, to the Nazi genocide.

Adult
(cont.)

Mosse, George. *Nazi Culture: A Documentary History.* New York: Schocken, 1981.

While primarily an anthology of original source material, Mosse includes a lengthy personal introduction, as well as introductions to each section and selection. Selections include material taken from speeches, newspapers, contemporary literature, and diaries.

Noakes, J., and G. Pridham, eds. *Nazism: A History in Documents and Eyewitness Accounts, 1919–1945* [2 vols.]. New York: Schocken, 1990.

This comprehensive work includes a wide range of official, government and party documents, newspapers, speeches, memoirs, letters, and diaries. The first volume covers the Nazis' rise to power and the domestic aspects of their regime from 1933 to 1939. Volume two examines foreign policy in the prewar and war periods, the occupation of Poland, the euthanasia program, and the implementation of the genocide policies.

Plant, Richard. *The Pink Triangle: The Nazi War against Homosexuals.* New York: Henry Holt, 1986.

The Nazis condemned homosexuals as "socially aberrant." Soon after Hitler came to power in 1933, Storm Troopers raided nightclubs and other places where homosexuals met. About 10,000 people were imprisoned as homosexuals, and many of them perished in concentration camps. In the camps, homosexuals' uniforms sometimes bore a pink triangular badge as an identifying mark. In this volume, the first comprehensive study available in English, Plant examines the ideological motivations for the Nazi persecution of homosexuals and the history of the implementation of Nazi policies.

Roth, John K., and Michael Berenbaum, eds. *The Holocaust: Religious and Philosophical Implications.* New York: Paragon House, 1989.

In this useful collection of over twenty previously published essays by many of the leading Holocaust scholars, the writers offer a range of responses to difficult questions concerning the uniqueness of the Holocaust and the impact of the catastrophe on Jewish religious beliefs.

Rubenstein, Richard L. *The Cunning of History.* New York: HarperCollins, 1987.

This slim volume is less a history of the Holocaust than an extended essay that attempts to put the Holocaust into historical perspective. Rubenstein's original but controversial tenet essentially describes the Holocaust as the culmination of twentieth-century technology and bureaucracy.

Adult
(cont.)

Taylor, Telford. *The Anatomy of the Nuremberg Trials: A Personal Memoir.* New York: Alfred A. Knopf, 1992.

Telford Taylor was a member of the American prosecution staff at the Nuremberg trials and eventually became chief counsel. This is a detailed, fascinating account of the inner workings of the trials and the behavior of the defendants and many other participants, both inside and outside the courtroom.

Tec, Nechama. *When Light Pierced the Darkness: Christian Rescue of Jews in Nazi-Occupied Poland.* New York: Oxford University Press, 1987.

Tec studied those who risked their lives to save Jews in an attempt to find a sociological pattern, to determine what characteristics these people had in common, whether they were related by class, religion, or other factors.

Wyman, David S. *The Abandonment of the Jews.* New York: Pantheon, 1986.

Wyman asks and answers the basic questions about how much was known in America about the "Final Solution." In addition to his criticism of the official response from the United States government in general, and from President Roosevelt in particular, Wyman also indicts some of the American Zionist leaders.

3. BIOGRAPHY

Baker, Leonard. *Days of Sorrow and Pain: Leo Baeck and the Berlin Jews.* New York: Oxford University Press, 1980.

Leo Baeck was the leading rabbi in Berlin when Hitler came to power, and he assumed a main role in helping Berlin Jews, first to emigrate and, when that was no longer possible, to resist through underground activities. Refusing to leave Germany himself, he eventually was sent to Theresienstadt.

Breitman, Richard. *The Architect of Genocide: Himmler and the Final Solution.* New York: Alfred A. Knopf, 1991.

This is not a biography of Himmler in the traditional sense that it chronicles the life of the man from birth to death. Rather, it focuses on his years as a Nazi, his relationship with Hitler, and his role in masterminding the "Final Solution." Other Nazi leaders, like Goering and Goebbels, are discussed at length.

Adult
(cont.)

Breitman, Richard, and Walter Laqueur. *Breaking the Silence: The Man Who Exposed the Final Solution.* **Hanover, NH: University Press of New England, 1986.**

Eduard Schulte was a major German industrialist who abhorred Hitler and Nazism. He is the man credited with passing on to the Allies news not only of troop movements and weapon programs but of the Nazi plans for genocide. This biography relates Schulte's story from his childhood to his postwar years. The authors also describe the responses of Allied governments to the information he passed on to them.

Bullock, Alan. *Hitler: A Study in Tyranny.* **New York: HarperCollins, 1991.**

The focus of this study is less on Hitler himself than on his position within the Nazi Party. Bullock explores the connection between Hitler and Nazism and places both in historical context. In addition, he traces the roots of Nazism back to the Weimar Republic.

Keneally, Thomas. *Schindler's List.* **New York: Simon and Schuster, 1992.**

Oskar Schindler was an influential German industrialist with high-level connections in Nazi Germany. He used his position to protect many Jews. Keneally's absorbing biography is based on interviews with many of those helped by Schindler.

Sereny, Gitta. *Into that Darkness.* **New York: Random House, 1983.**

Franz Stangl, a convicted Nazi war criminal, was interviewed in prison by the author. These interviews are supplemented by testimony from witnesses. Stangl was commandant of the camps at both Sobibor and Treblinka. His testimony, as told to Sereny, is revealing and chilling.

4. FICTION

Appelfeld, Aharon. *Badenheim, 1939.* **New York: Pocket Books, 1981.**

The story revolves around a group of upper-class Jews in an Austrian resort town, on the eve of war. The author, himself a Holocaust survivor, creates a haunting picture of impending tragedy, heightened by the reader's awareness of the events to come.

Adult
(cont.)

Begley, Louis. *Wartime Lies*. New York: David McKay, 1991.

Begley, himself a child caught up in the Holocaust, has written a first-person novel about a young Jewish boy and his aunt who survive only due to a pattern of denial and compromise that leaves its own scars.

Borowski, Tadeusz. *This Way for the Gas, Ladies and Gentlemen*. New York: Viking Penguin, 1992.

Through this collection of remarkable short stories, Borowski describes his experiences in Auschwitz and Dachau. His focus is on the atmosphere of the camps and its effect on the inner being. He probes the minds of both victims and perpetrators.

Fink, Ida. *A Scrap of Time*. New York: Schocken, 1989.

The title story in this collection of short stories concerns the way time was measured by Holocaust victims. Other stories describe people in a variety of normal human situations distorted by the circumstances of the times.

Friedlander, Albert. *Out of the Whirlwind*. New York: Schocken, 1989.

Not all of the entries in this anthology are fiction; excerpts are also included from historical works and personal narratives. The book is arranged thematically, making it especially helpful for a teacher looking for material to support specific aspects of a curriculum.

Glatstein, Jacob. *Anthology of Holocaust Literature*. New York: Macmillan, 1973.

Chapters in this collection cover life in the ghettos, children, the camps, resistance, and non-Jewish victims. Excerpts are included from both works of fiction and primary source materials such as diaries, memoirs, and ghetto documents. Many of these pieces can be especially useful if teachers provide additional background information on the authors and context of the writings.

Kosinski, Jerzy. *The Painted Bird*. New York: Random House, 1983.

In this autobiographical novel, Kosinski chronicles the horrors visited upon a six-year-old boy wandering through Europe during the Holocaust. This is without doubt the most graphic and brutal Holocaust material in existence.

Adult
(cont.)

Ozick, Cynthia. *The Shawl*. New York: Random House, 1990.

Originally published as two separate stories in *The New Yorker*, the first, very brief, title story tells of a mother witnessing her baby's death at the hands of camp guards. The second story, "Rose," describes that same mother 30 years later, still haunted by that event. This is Holocaust fiction at its best, brief but unforgettable.

Schwarz-Bart, André. *The Last of the Just*. Cambridge, MA: Robert Bentley, 1981.

Based on the Talmudic legend of thirty-six men of each generation upon whose virtue the existence of the world depends, this novel traces the history of the Levy family from medieval times to Ernie Levy, the last of the just, who died at Auschwitz.

Wiesel, Elie. *The Town Beyond the Wall*. New York: Schocken, 1982.

In this post-Holocaust novel, a survivor returns to his hometown seeking to understand and confront those who stood by and watched his deportation. Wiesel probes the issue of survivors coming to terms with the Holocaust experience.

5. MEMOIRS

Anatoli, A. *Babi Yar: A Document in the Form of a Novel*. Cambridge, MA: Robert Bentley, 1979.

As a Russian boy of twelve, A. Anatoli used to play in the Babi Yar ravine near Kiev and was in earshot of the machine gun fire that signaled the massacre by Nazi mobile killing units of more than 33,000 Jews on September 29 and 30, 1941. Long regarded as one of the greatest Soviet novels of World War II, *Babi Yar* is an unforgettable account of the years of German occupation.

Delbo, Charlotte. *None of Us Will Survive*. Boston: Beacon Press, 1968.

Delbo is one of the most eloquent of Holocaust writers. She writes of her experiences at Auschwitz in prose so powerful that the reader seems to become a part of the experience. Through the poetic use of language rather than graphic descriptions of atrocities, she creates unforgettable images.

*Adult
(cont.)*   **Donat, Alexander. *The Holocaust Kingdom*. New York: Anti-Defamation League, 1963.**

The author, a Polish Jew whose Holocaust experiences included the Warsaw ghetto, Majdanek, and Dachau, was separated from his wife and son at Majdanek but reunited with them after the war. He tells his own story and the stories of others with whom he came in contact. His wife describes her own experiences in the final section of the book.

Eliach, Yaffa. *Hasidic Tales of the Holocaust*. New York: Vintage Books, 1988.

Through interviews and oral histories, Eliach garnered eighty-nine tales, both true stories and fanciful legends. This beautiful, compelling collection bears witness, in a traditional idiom, to the victims' suffering, dying, and surviving.

Frankl, Viktor. *Man's Search for Meaning: An Introduction to Logotherapy*. New York: Pocket Books, 1984.

A psychiatrist as well as a concentration camp survivor, Frankl's work is only secondarily a personal memoir. Primarily, it is an attempt to understand and explain the psychology of camp victims through Frankl's own experiences and observations.

Hillesum, Etty. *An Interrupted Life*. New York: Pocket Books, 1991.

Hillesum's diary entries from 1941–42 and her letters to family and friends from the Westerbork transit camp in occupied Netherlands reveal her personal development in a time of terror. Soon after being deported from Westerbork, she died in Auschwitz, at the age of twenty-nine.

Leitner, Isabella. *Fragments of Isabella: A Memoir of Auschwitz*. New York: Dell, 1983.

A survivor of Auschwitz recounts the ordeal of holding her family together after their mother is killed in the camp. This slim volume is an eloquent account of survival in the midst of chaos and destruction. A glossary of camp language is a valuable addition. Leitner's story is continued in *Saving the Fragments*.

Levi, Primo. *Survival in Auschwitz*. New York: Macmillan, 1987.

Levi was an Italian Jew captured in 1943 and still at Auschwitz at the time of liberation. He not only chronicles the daily activities in the camp, but his inner reactions to it and the destruction of the inner as well as the outer self. This memoir is one of the most important books on the Holocaust.

Adult
(cont.)

Meed, Vladka. *On Both Sides of the Wall.* New York: Holocaust Publications, 1979.

This is an informative memoir of the Warsaw ghetto by one of the young smugglers who maintained contact between the ghetto and the Aryan side of the city. Working for the Jewish Combat Organization (ZOB), Vladka Meed helped smuggle weapons and ammunition into the ghetto.

Nir, Yehuda. *The Lost Childhood.* San Diego: Harcourt Brace Jovanovich, 1991.

This compelling memoir chronicles six extraordinary years in the life of a Polish Jewish boy, his mother, and his sister, who all survived the Holocaust by obtaining false papers and posing as Catholics. Yehuda Nir lost almost everything, including his father, his possessions, his youth and innocence, and his identity, but he managed to live with the help of chance, personal resourcefulness, and the support of his family.

Szwajger, Adina B. *I Remember Nothing More: The Warsaw Children's Hospital and the Jewish Resistance.* New York: Simon and Schuster, 1992.

The author was beginning her last year of medical school when the Nazis invaded Poland in 1939. From that time until January 1943, she worked in the Children's Hospital of the Warsaw ghetto. When the hospital was closed after the first armed Jewish resistance, she left the ghetto with false papers and, from then until the liberation, worked as a courier for the resistance.

Wiesel, Elie. *Night.* New York: Bantam, 1960.

Wiesel is one of the most eloquent writers of the Holocaust, and this book is his best-known work. This compelling narrative describes his own experience in Auschwitz. His account of his entrance into Auschwitz and his first night in the camp is extraordinary. This narrative is often considered required reading for students of the Holocaust.

Yoors, Jan. *Crossing: A Journal of Survival and Resistance in World War II.* New York: Simon and Schuster, 1971.

Every summer during his teen years, Yoors left his comfortable, upper-middle-class family life in Belgium to travel around Europe with a Rom (Gypsy) family. This beautifully written journal focuses on the participation of Yoors and his fondly remembered Rom friends in resistance activities during World War II.

6. DIARIES

Frank, Anne. *The Diary of Anne Frank: The Critical Edition*. New York: Doubleday and Company, 1989.

This edition of the internationally acclaimed diary includes three different versions: the portion that was originally found, the revisions made by Anne herself, and the version edited by her father. In addition, there is extensive commentary on each version.

Hilberg, Raul, et al., eds. *The Warsaw Diary of Adam Czerniakow*. Lanham, MD: Madison Books, 1982.

Czerniakow was chairman of the Nazi-appointed Jewish Council in Warsaw from the German invasion in 1939 until his suicide in 1942. His diaries record the history of the period as well as his personal involvement with the Germans.

Ringelblum, Emmanuel. *Notes from the Warsaw Ghetto: The Journal of Emmanuel Ringelblum*. New York: Schocken, 1974.

The official archivist of the Warsaw ghetto, Ringelblum's training as a historian made him uniquely qualified to understand the importance of documenting events inside the ghetto. He carefully collected and hid documentary evidence and personal notes.

Tory, Avraham. *Surviving the Holocaust: The Kovno Ghetto Diary*. Cambridge, MA: Harvard University Press, 1990.

Tory, a ghetto inmate and secretary of the Jewish Council, wrote this account under conditions of extreme danger. This remarkable, detailed chronicle documents life and death in the Jewish ghetto of Kovno, Lithuania, from June 1941 to January 1944. Translated from the Yiddish, the book includes a valuable collection of photos and sketches by artists in the ghetto.

7. POETRY, DRAMA, AND ART

Fuchs, Elinor, ed. *Plays of the Holocaust: An International Anthology*. New York: Theater Communications Group, 1987.

The author has selected plays from a variety of nations in a number of literary styles. In addition to the plays themselves, the book includes a bibliography of Holocaust drama.

Adult
(cont.)

Heyen, William. *Erika: Poems of the Holocaust.* St. Louis, MO: Time Being Books, 1991.

Heyen and his immediate family immigrated to the United States from Germany before the war, but he had two uncles who remained there and died serving Germany. Heyen's poems reflect his unique perspective and his ambivalent feelings about his family's painful history. Earlier editions were published under the title *Swastika Poems.*

Hinz, Berthold. *Art in the Third Reich.* New York: Pantheon, 1979.

The art and architecture produced during the Third Reich is examined not only for its content and technique, but for the role it played in Nazi politics and philosophy. Numerous reproductions supplement the text.

Hyett, Barbara Helfgott. *In Evidence: Poems of the Liberation of Nazi Concentration Camps.* Pittsburgh: University of Pittsburgh Press, 1986.

Part of a team that interviewed American liberators of concentration camps, Hyett translated their words into these poems. The selections are brief and the language is spare and stark, reflecting the difficulty these men had in articulating the horrors they witnessed.

Skloot, Robert, ed. *The Theater of the Holocaust: Four Plays.* Madison: University of Wisconsin Press, 1982.

The four plays by Shimon Wincelberg, Harold and Edith Lieberman, George Tabori, and Charlotte Delbo reflect a range of stylistic and artistic approaches. Together, they constitute an eloquent testimony to the possibility of survival during times of extreme oppression and human degradation.

8. LITERARY CRITICISM

Aaron, Frieda W. *Bearing the Unbearable: Yiddish and Polish Poetry in the Ghettos and Concentration Camps.* Albany, NY: State University of New York Press, 1990.

Aaron, herself a survivor of the Warsaw ghetto and Majdanek concentration camp, has undertaken the first study of Yiddish and Polish camp poetry. She emphasizes the distinction between contemporary writings and works written after the experience, the latter typical of most Holocaust literature.

Adult (cont.)   **Ezrahi, Sidra D. *By Words Alone: The Holocaust in Literature*. Chicago: University of Chicago Press, 1982.**

This literary history of the Holocaust discusses a number of specific works, including works in American literature. The author also focuses on the language of the Holocaust and the ways in which different writers interpret the same facts.

Fine, Ellen. *The Legacy of Night: The Literary Universe of Elie Wiesel*. Albany, NY: State University of New York Press, 1983.

Fine looks closely at the works of Wiesel, tracing the literary and spiritual patterns she finds. In addition to looking at connections between books, from *Night* to *The Testament*, she examines individual books in depth. Other works on Wiesel include *The Vision of the Void* by Michael Berenbaum and *Confronting the Holocaust* edited by Alvin Rosenfeld and Irving Greenberg.

Heinemann, Marlene E. *Gender and Destiny: Women Writers and the Holocaust*. Westport, CT: Greenwood Publishing Group, 1986.

Focusing on six specific Holocaust books by women writers, including Charlotte Delbo's *None of Us Will Return,* Heinemann examines the areas in which Holocaust literature by female writers differs from that created by male writers.

Insdorf, Annette. *Indelible Shadows: Film and the Holocaust*. New York: Cambridge University Press, 1990.

Films from both Hollywood and Germany are examined here, as well as films produced in other, mostly western, European countries. Both documentaries and fictional films are included, as are both short and feature-length films. Insdorf particularly looks at whether a film confronts or evades the real issues of the Holocaust.

Langer, Lawrence L. *The Age of Atrocity: Death in Modern Literature*. Boston: Beacon Press, 1978.

In this study, Langer analyzes four major literary works, by Mann, Camus, Solzhenitsyn, and Delbo. Using these works as examples, he traces the evolution of the twentieth-century concept of death, from individual death to mass death to death by atrocity and death by extermination. From both literary and historical perspectives, this book contributes a great deal to the understanding of the Holocaust and of "inappropriate death."

Adult
(cont.)

Langer, Lawrence L. *The Holocaust and the Literary Imagination.* New Haven, CT: Yale University Press, 1975.

Examining specific literary works, Langer provides detailed analysis of a number of novels, including Schwarz-Bart's *The Last of the Just* and Kosinki's *The Painted Bird.* He also includes some poetry and Wiesel's *Night,* which, although nonfiction, qualifies as literature due to its "imaginative power and artful presentation."

Rosenfeld, Alvin H. *A Double Dying: Reflections on Holocaust Literature.* Bloomington, IN: Indiana University Press, 1980.

This survey of Holocaust literature includes works of both fiction and nonfiction. Rosenfeld focuses particularly on the criteria for judging books on the Holocaust. He discusses a number of individual books, from classics like *Night* to more recent works, including some which he describes as exploiting the Holocaust. The usefulness of this source is augmented by an excellent bibliography.

Roskies, David. *Against the Apocalypse: Responses to Catastrophe in Modern Jewish Culture.* Cambridge, MA: Harvard University, 1984.

This scholarly study of Jewish literature includes both pre- and post-Holocaust literature in addition to Holocaust literature itself. It also includes monuments and other works of art. It focuses on the literary and artistic expression of modern Jewish experience in eastern Europe, beginning in the late nineteenth century and continuing through World War I and the Holocaust into the post-Holocaust world.

Index of Books
by Author

Appelfeld, Aharon. *Badenheim, 1939*, 48

————. *To the Land of the Cattails*, 32

Arad, Yitzhak. *Ghetto in Flames*, 28

Atkinson, Linda. *In Kindling Flame: The Story of Hannah Senesh 1921–1944*, 21

Auerbacher, Inge. *I Am a Star: Child of the Holocaust*, 23

Bachrach, Susan D. *Tell Them We Remember: The Story of the Holocaust*, 19

Baker, Leonard. *Days of Sorrow and Pain: Leo Baeck and the Berlin Jews*, 47

Bartoszewski, Wladyslaw T. *The Warsaw Ghetto: A Christian's Testimony*, 39

Bauer, Yehuda, and Nili Keren. *A History of the Holocaust*, 27

Bauer, Yehuda, and Nathan Rotenstreich, eds. *The Holocaust as Historical Experience*, 39

Begley, Louis. *Wartime Lies*, 49

Berenbaum, Michael. *The World Must Know: A History of the Holocaust as Told in the United States Holocaust Memorial Museum*, 36

————, ed. *A Mosaic of Victims: Non-Jews Persecuted and Murdered by the Nazis*, 39

Bernbaum, Israel. *My Brother's Keeper: The Holocaust Through the Eyes of an Artist*, 26

Bernheim, Mark. *Father of the Orphans: The Story of Janusz Korczak*, 21

Bierman, John. *Righteous Gentile: The Story of Raoul Wallenberg, Missing Hero of the Holocaust*, 31

Block, Gay, and Malka Drucker. *Rescuers: Portraits of Moral Courage in the Holocaust*, 29

Borowski, Tadeusz. *This Way for the Gas, Ladies and Gentlemen*, 49

Breitman, Richard. *The Architect of Genocide: Himmler and the Final Solution*, 47

Breitman, Richard, and Walter Laqueur. *Breaking the Silence: The Man Who Exposed the Final Solution*, 31, 48

Bridenthal, Renate, et al. *When Biology Became Destiny: Women in Weimar and Nazi Germany*, 39

Browning, Christopher. *Ordinary Men: Reserve Battalion 101 and the Final Solution in Poland*, 39

Bullock, Alan. *Hitler: A Study in Tyranny*, 48

Burleigh, Michael, and Wolfgang Wipperman. *The Racial State: Germany 1933–1945*, 40

Chaikin, Miriam. *A Nightmare in History: The Holocaust 1933–1945*, 19

Gallagher, Hugh Gregory. *By Trust Betrayed: Patients, Physicians, and the License to Kill in the Third Reich*, 42

Gehrts, Barbara. *Don't Say a Word*, 22

Gellately, Robert. *The Gestapo and German Society: Enforcing Racial Policy*, 42

Gies, Miep, and Alison L. Gold. *Anne Frank Remembered: The Story of the Woman Who Helped to Hide the Frank Family*, 34

Gilbert, Martin. *The Holocaust: A History of the Jews in Europe during the Second World War*, 27, 37

Glatstein, Jacob. *Anthology of Holocaust Literature*, 33, 49

Gurdus, Luba K. *The Death Train*, 34

Gutman, Yisrael, and Michael Berenbaum, eds. *Anatomy of the Auschwitz Death Camp*, 42

Hayes, Peter, ed. *Lessons and Legacies: The Meaning of the Holocaust in a Changing World*, 37

Heinemann, Marlene E. *Gender and Destiny: Women Writers and the Holocaust*, 55

Herzstein, Robert E. *Roosevelt and Hitler: Prelude to War*, 42

————. *The War that Hitler Won: Goebbels and the Nazi Media Campaign*, 42

Heyen, William. *Erika: Poems of the Holocaust*, 54

Hilberg, Raul. *The Destruction of the European Jews* [3 vols.], 37

————. *The Destruction of the European Jews* [student text], 27

————. *Perpetrators, Victims, Bystanders: the Jewish Catastrophe, 1933–1945*, 27

Hilberg, Raul, et al., eds. *The Warsaw Diary of Adam Czerniakow*, 53

Hillesum, Etty. *An Interrupted Life*, 51

Hinz, Berthold. *Art in the Third Reich*, 54

Horwitz, Gordon. *In the Shadow of Death: Living Outside the Gates of Mauthausen*, 43

Hyett, Barbara Helfgott. *In Evidence: Poems of the Liberation of Nazi Concentration Camps*, 54

Innocenti, Roberto. *Rose Blanche*, 26

Insdorf, Annette. *Indelible Shadows: Film and the Holocaust*, 55

Isaacman, Clara, and Joan A. Grossman. *Clara's Story*, 24

Josephs, Jeremy. *Swastika Over Paris: The Fate of the Jews in France*, 30

Kamenetsky, Christa. *Children's Literature in Hitler's Germany: The Cultural Policy of National Socialism*, 43

A N N O T A T E D   V I D E O G R A P H Y

This annotated videography has been designed to identify videotapes addressing Holocaust history that have been used effectively in classrooms. Today, many schools purchase or rent videotapes and videocassettes instead of films, which are more expensive and cumbersome to use. An increasing number of educators rely on videotaped documentaries when teaching the Holocaust.

The titles listed here have been chosen both because of their individual merit and because most of them are readily available. Many excellent videotapes are not on this list because they are too difficult to obtain. Most annotations suggest a distributor from whom educators can purchase their own tapes, although the availability and distribution can change. Many of the videos may be purchased by phone and mail order from the U.S. Holocaust Memorial Museum Shop (100 Raoul Wallenberg Place, SW, Washington, DC 20024-2150; tel. 202-488-6144. Schools receive a 10% discount). Alternatively, educators can rent or borrow the videotapes from Holocaust resource centers, libraries, and schools.

A main concern of educators using audio-visual materials on the Holocaust is that graphic footage depicting people who were starved, tortured, or killed can be upsetting to viewers of all ages. Videotaped eyewitness testimonies often contain vivid descriptions of the horrors encountered by victims. When the horror is presented, it should be done in a sensitive manner, and only to the extent necessary to achieve the objective of the lesson.

In any study of the Holocaust, the sheer number of victims challenges easy comprehension. Video footage can remind students that individual people—families of grandparents, parents, and children—are behind the statistics. The first-person accounts and stories contained in many of the videotapes provide students with a context for studying collective numbers. Although students should be careful about overgeneralizing from first-person accounts such as those from survivors, journalists, relief workers, bystanders, and liberators, these individual stories help students get beyond statistics and make historical events of the Holocaust more immediate.

This videography includes recommendations for use at the middle school and high school levels. Many of the videos are appropriate for both levels, while others have been recommended for just high school students. Videos recommended for older students usually present concepts or topics too complex for younger students, who often lack awareness of the relevant history needed to understand the information presented.

In choosing a videotape, teachers should consider the length of the videotape and the density of the information presented. Some videotapes on this list require a considerable commitment of time; the longest is the ten-hour documentary *Shoah*. Other videos such as *Das Leben von Adolf Hitler (The Life of Adolf Hitler)* or *Auschwitz and the Allies* contain a great deal of historical information and should be viewed in segments.

Educators indicate that most students are engaged by the videotapes listed in this pamphlet and that they want to discuss what they have viewed. Most students demonstrate a high level of interest in studying the Holocaust precisely because the subject raises questions of fairness, justice, individual identity, peer pressure, conformity, indifference, and obedience—issues that adolescents tend to confront in their daily lives. Students are also struck by the magnitude of the Holocaust, and the fact that so many people allowed this genocide to occur by acting as collaborators or perpetrators or by failing to protest or resist as bystanders.

The videotapes on this list have been classified as documentaries, survivor testimonies, animation, docu-dramas, or dramas. In addition, three films not specifically about the Holocaust have been included: *The Wave*; *The Hangman*; and *Obedience: The Milgram Experiment*. Although some educators question the value of using these films within the context of a course on the Holocaust, many educators have found these films useful in providing students with a vocabulary for examining human behavior and in addressing social studies concepts such as obedience, victims, victimizers, bystanders, and peer pressure.

As a general rule, this videography does not recommend the use of "docu-dramas," which use dramatic license to recreate historical events. Nevertheless, four docu-dramas, *Korczak*, *The Wannsee Conference*, *Au Revoir les Enfants (Goodbye, Children)*, and *Schindler's List*, have been selected on their merits. A fifth docu-drama, *Murderers Among Us: The Simon Wiesenthal Story*, can accompany the reading of the book *The Sunflower*. When showing any docu-drama, educators should remind viewers that the film is a fictional account of historic events.

While videos may capture and isolate an event or a memory for the historical record, viewers should be reminded that not even documentary footage is neutral. The subjective process of selection and editing is basic to filmmaking; the decision to record something can and does alter what we see or do not see. If students are aware of this bias of selection, it can help them to analyze events from various vantage points.

For example, a good deal of documentary footage was filmed by the Nazis, often for propaganda purposes. Students can gain more sophisticated insights into the history if they examine some of the motives behind recording and producing a particular film. They should be encouraged to ask why a particular scene was filmed, or how people in the film responded to having their pictures taken. Many people filmed by the Nazis were obviously under duress.

Documentary footage was also taken by camp liberators at the end of World War II. Many of these soldiers had endured the hardships of war and had seen evidence of Nazi atrocities throughout Europe. Thus, these filmmakers brought their own perspectives to their work.

Condensed accounts of the Holocaust which continually show people only as victims can in themselves be dehumanizing. Where time permits, showing a video that captures life before the Holocaust provides a useful balance. Students may better understand the dimensions of the tragedy when they see the richness and diversity of life in Europe before the Holocaust. By showing images of children and their families in the kinds of situations captured on home video today, such as vacations, holidays, weddings, and school graduations, these types of films help students identify and empathize with the victims.

Where a teacher has been unable to arrange for a survivor to meet with students in person, an alternative is the use of videos which feature survivor testimony. Hearing someone speak about his or her own experiences during the Holocaust helps to personalize an event beyond the often numbing statistics, and is another way to promote students' identification with and empathy for the victims.

The videography that follows lists videotapes by topics, beginning with videos that provide a general overview of the Holocaust. The topics are generally arranged in chronological order, beginning with videos on life before the Holocaust and continuing through ghettos and camps, to rescue, resistance, and liberation, to post-Holocaust subjects, including the war crimes trials. The videography concludes with videos on subjects related to but not directly addressing the Holocaust. An index to all annotated videos by title and subject may be found after the annotations.

Key

D	Documentary	DR	Drama
ST	Survivor Testimony	b/w	Black and White
DD	Docu-Drama	c	Color
A	Animation	CC	Closed Captioned

Overviews
of the Holocaust

Genocide, 1941–1945 (World At War Series)   [D] [c] [b/w] 00:50:00

Source: Zenger Video, 10200 Jefferson Blvd., P.O. Box 802, Culver City, CA 90232-0802; 800-421-4246. #SV2
Credits: Produced and directed by Michael Darlow. 1982.
Recommended for Middle School, High School, and Adult.

The story of the destruction of European Jewry is told using archival footage and testimonies of victims, perpetrators, and bystanders. This excellent overview has been used effectively by many teachers.

Shoah   [ST] [c]

(Part 1) 02:00:00; (2) 02:00:00; (3) 01:50:00; (4) 02:00:00; (5) 01:56:00
Source: Available in most video stores and many libraries. Also may be purchased from the Simon Wiesenthal Center, 9760 West Pico Blvd., Yeshiva University of Los Angeles, Los Angeles, CA 90035; 310-553-9036.
Credits: Directed by Claude Lanzmann. 1985.
Recommended for High School and Adult.

This powerful film includes interviews with victims, perpetrators, and bystanders, and takes us to the locations of the Holocaust in camps, towns, and railways. The video may be segmented for classroom use.

Witness to the Holocaust   [D] [b/w] 02:10:00 *(Two video set)*

Source: ADL, 823 United Nations Plaza, New York, NY 10017.
Credits: Produced by the Holocaust Education Project for Zachor: National Jewish Resource Center. Produced and directed by C.J. Pressma. 1984.
Recommended for Middle School, High School, and Adult.

This video presents a series of seven documentaries which can easily be segmented for specific topical use in the classroom. Each segment is approximately 20 minutes in length. Survivor narration is combined with photos and historic film footage. The topics include: Rise of the Nazis, Ghetto Life, Deportations, Resistance, The Final Solution, Liberation, Reflections.

Life before the
Holocaust

Image Before My Eyes

D | c | b/w | 01:30:00

Source: Simon Wiesenthal Center, 9760 West Pico Blvd., Yeshiva University of Los Angeles, Los Angeles, CA 90035; 310-553-9036.
Credits: YIVO Institute for Jewish Research. Produced by Josh Waletzky, Susan Lazarus. 1980.
Recommended for Middle School, High School, and Adult.

Using photographs, drawings, home movies, music, and interviews with survivors, this documentary recreates Jewish life in Poland from the late nineteenth century up to the time of its destruction during the Holocaust. The diversity of the culture is examined as well as its achievements.

The Camera of My Family:
Four Generations in Germany 1845–1945

D | c | b/w | 00:20:00

Source: Zenger Video, 10200 Jefferson Blvd., P.O. Box 802, Culver City, CA 90232-0802; 800-421-4246. #ADL45V-J4.
Credits: Anti-Defamation League. 1991.
Recommended for Middle School and High School.

Catherine Hanf Noren left Nazi Germany with her Jewish parents shortly after her birth in 1938. This effective film describes her perseverance as an adult to use old family photographs to trace her family roots through several generations. Includes guide.

The Last Chapter

D | b/w | 01:25:00

Source: Ben-Lar Productions, 245 8th Ave., New York, NY 10011; 800-423-6527.
Credits: Produced and directed by Benjamin and Lawrence Rothman.
Recommended for Middle School, High School, and Adult.

This thorough and artistic documentary traces the history of the earliest Jewish communities in Poland through their destruction during World War II. It also examines the pogroms in the postwar period which occurred as survivors tried to return to Poland and rebuild their lives.

Perpetrators

Das Leben von Adolf Hitler (The Life of Adolf Hitler)

D | b/w | 01:51:00

Source: Video Yesteryear, Box C, Sandy Hook, CT 06482; 800-243-0987. #852.
Credits: Directed by Paul Rotha. 1961.
Recommended for Middle School, High School, and Adult.

Using archival footage, this film moves chronologically through the major events from the rise of the Nazis to their defeat by the Allies. It could be segmented for classroom use into three periods: 1933–36, 1936–39, and 1939–45.

A New Germany 1933–1939 (The World at War Series)   `D` `b/w` `c` 00:52:00

Source: Zenger Video, 10200 Jefferson Blvd., P.O. Box 802, Culver City, CA 90232-0802; 800-421-4246. #SV251V-J5.
Credits: Written and directed by Michael Darlow. 1975.
Recommended for Middle School, High School, and Adult.

This video traces the rise of Hitler to power and Nazi racism and antisemitic policies before the war. Photo stills and film footage are complemented by the testimonies of survivors and German perpetrators. The development and role of the Nazis' elite SS corps is highlighted.

The Wannsee Conference   `DD` `c` 01:26:49

Source: Zenger Video, 10200 Jefferson Blvd., P.O. Box 802, Culver City, CA 90232-0802; 800-421-4246. #SV443V.
Credits: Directed by Heinz Schirk. Co-production of Infafilm GmbH Munich; Manfred Korytowski, Austrian Television O.R.F.; and Bavarian Broadcasting Corporation. 1984.
Recommended for Middle School and High School.

The video dramatizes the famous conference where the leading Nazis discussed the implementation of the "Final Solution" by the German bureaucracy. An excellent film, it is in German with English subtitles.

Hitler: The Whole Story   `D` `b/w` 00:50:00 / 2:30:00

Source: NDR International. Hitler Offer: call 800-423-8800, or write Hitler Offer, P.O. Box 68618, Indianapolis, IN 46268.
Credits: Produced by Weiner Rieb and directed by Joachim C. Fest and Christian Herrendoerfer. 1989.
Recommended for Middle School, High School, and Adult.

Based on Joachim C. Fest's book *Hitler,* the film combines rare footage, photographs, and interviews. This film can be segmented into three parts for classroom use: Germany's quest for land, the "New Man" and Germania—a vision of the future, and deportations and mass killings.

Heil Hitler! Confessions of a Hitler Youth
D | b/w | c | 00:30:00

Source: Zenger Video, 10200 Jefferson Blvd., P.O. Box 802, Culver City, CA 90232-0802; 800-421-4246. #TL338V-J4.
Credits: HBO. 1991.
Recommended for Middle School, High School, and Adult.

Eloquent Alfons Heck, a former member of Hitler Youth and now a U.S. citizen dedicated to Holocaust education, recounts the compelling story of how he became a fanatic supporter of Nazism. Documentary footage vividly demonstrates how songs, youth camps, speeches, and education turned millions of young Germans like Heck into the most fervent and loyal proponents of Nazi racism and militarism. The short length of this highly recommended film makes it especially suitable for classroom use.

The Democrat and the Dictator
D | b/w | c | 00:55:00

Source: PBS Videos, 1320 Braddock Place, Alexandria, VA 22314-1698; 800-344-3337.
Credits: Produced by Betsy McCarthy. 1984.
Recommended for High School and Adult.

This film is a part of *A Second Look with Bill Moyers* and compares the personal history and style of the two major political leaders of the twentieth century, Adolf Hitler and Franklin Delano Roosevelt.

Racism, Antisemitism

The Longest Hatred: The History of Anti-Semitism
D | c | CC | 02:30:00

Source: Films for the Humanities and Sciences, Inc., Box 2053, Princeton, NJ 08543; 609-275-1400.
Credits: Thames Television and WGBH Educational Foundation. 1993.
Recommended for High School and Adult.

Drawing on interviews with Jews and antisemites as well as prominent scholars in Europe, America, and the Middle East, this excellent video traces antisemitism from its earliest manifestations to recent outbreaks in Germany and Eastern Europe. This film can be segmented for classroom use.

Shadow on the Cross

D c   00:52:00

Source: Landmark Films Inc., 3450 Slade Run Drive, Falls Church, VA 22042; 800-342-4336.
Credits: CTVC Production for Channel 4, England. Produced by Ray Bruce. 1990.
Recommended for High School and Adult.

This documentary film looks at the tragic story of Jewish-Christian relations over the past 2000 years and explores the influences of historic Christian anti-semitism on the Third Reich. The film is divided into two parts. Part 1 summarizes the history of religious antisemitism over the two thousand years Jews lived in Europe as a religious minority. In Part 2 theologians discuss the implications of the Holocaust for Jewish-Christian relations today. This is useful for college or high school history, political science, religion, or philosophy classes.

Of Pure Blood

D b/w c   01:40:00

Source: No distributor currently available.
Credits: Produced by Maryse Addison and Peter Bate. A film by Clarissa Henry and Marc Hillel. 1972.
Recommended for High School and Adult.

Using historical film footage and interviews with some of Hitler's victims, this film chronicles the Nazis' attempts to create a "master race." This is an excellent film for examining the whole issue of eugenics and racism. It also helps answer the question, "How was Hitler representative of the master race when he failed to match the ideal of the tall, blond-haired, blue-eyed German?" One segment of this film portrays nudity.

Mosaic of Victims

More Than Broken Glass: Memories of Kristallnacht

D ST c   00:57:00

Source: Ergo Media Inc., P.O. Box 2037, Teaneck, NJ 07666. 800-695-3746. #616.
Credits: Written, produced, and directed by Chris Pelzer. 1988.
Recommended for High School and Adult.

Using archival footage, photographs, and interviews with survivors, Jewish life in Germany prior to and during the Holocaust is described. This is excellent for examining the persecution of German Jews.

One Survivor Remembers

D b/w c 00:36:00

Source: United States Holocaust Memorial Museum Shop, 100 Raoul Wallenberg Place, SW, Washington DC 20024-2150; 202-488-6144.
Credits: Home Box Office in association with the United States Holocaust Memorial Museum and Wentworth Films, Inc. 1995.
Recommended for High School and Adult.

> Survivor Gerda Weissmann Klein eloquently recounts the personal story of her life before the war in Poland, her Holocaust experiences, including the painful loss of most of her family, and the suffering she endured on a final "death march" near the end of the war. Her story is told in fuller detail in her autobiography *All But My Life.*

Persecuted and Forgotten

D ST c 00:54:00

Source: EBS Productions, 330 Ritch Street, San Francisco, CA 94107; 415-495-2327.
Credits: Medienwerkstatt Franken. 1989.
Recommended for High School and Adult.

> This video follows a group of German Gypsies as they return to Auschwitz after World War II. In personal accounts, Gypsies recall the "Gypsy Police," the Institute for Racial Hygiene, and the genealogical research that led to the imprisonment and murder of Gypsies during the Holocaust. The Gypsies who are interviewed also reveal the discrimination they continue to suffer.

Purple Triangles

D ST c 00:25:00

Source: Watchtower Bible and Tract Society of New York, Inc., 25 Columbia Heights, Brooklyn, NY 11201.
Credits: Produced and directed by Martin Smith. 1991.
Recommended for Middle School, High School, and Adult.

> During the Holocaust, Jehovah's Witnesses were persecuted as a religious group. Their story is told by surviving members of the Kusserow family who describe their arrest and incarceration in concentration camps, where they were identified by their purple triangles.

We Were Marked with a Big "A"   ☐D ☐c ☐b/w 00:44:00

Source: United States Holocaust Memorial Museum Shop, 100 Raoul Wallenberg Place, SW, Washington, DC 20024-2150; 202-488-6144.
Credits: Directed by Elke Jeanrond and Joseph Weishaupt. 1991.
Recommended for High School and Adult.

Little is known about the persecution of homosexuals by the Nazis. For the first time, in this effective documentary, three gay survivors tell the story of their arrests and incarceration in concentration camps. In German, with subtitles.

Korczak   ☐DD ☐b/w 02:00:00

Source: New York Films Video, 16 W. 61st Street, New York, NY 10023; 212-247-6110. Attn.: John Montague. Rental, 16 and 35mm.
Credits: Directed by Andrzej Wajda. 1990.
Recommended for High School and Adult.

Nominated for Best Foreign Film, this movie is based on the true story of a doctor who cared for 200 orphans in the Warsaw ghetto. Korczak refused offers of rescue for himself and insisted on remaining with the children as they were deported to their deaths at the Treblinka extermination camp. In Polish, with subtitles.

Ghettos   ### Lodz Ghetto   ☐D ☐c ☐b/w 01:43:00

Source: Alan Adelson, Exec. Dir., Jewish Heritage Project, Inc., 150 Franklin Street, #1W, New York, NY 10003; 212-925-9067.
Credits: Produced by Alan Adelson. Directed by Alan Adelson and Kathryn Taverna. 1989.
Recommended for Middle School, High School, and Adult.

This documentary recounts the history of one of the last ghettos to be liquidated. The film draws on written accounts by Jews in the Lodz ghetto and on photographs, slides, and rare film footage. A teacher's guide is available through the ADL, 823 U.N. Plaza, New York, NY 10017. The book *Lodz Ghetto: Inside a Community Under Seige* may be effectively paired with the video.

The Warsaw Ghetto

D b/w 00:51:00

Source: Zenger Video, 10200 Jefferson Blvd., P.O. Box 802, Culver City, CA 90232-0802; 800-421-4246. #BV103V.
Credits: B.B.C. Production. 1969.
Recommended for Middle School, High School, and Adult.

Narrated by a ghetto survivor, this documentary uses historic film footage made by the Nazis and shows the creation of the ghetto, early Nazi propaganda, scenes from everyday life, and the final weeks of resistance before the ghetto was liquidated.

Camps ### Auschwitz: If You Cried, You Died

D c b/w 00:28:00

Source: Impact America Foundation, Inc. c/o Martin J. Moore, 9100 Keystone at the Crossing, Suite 390, Indianapolis, IN 46240-2158; 317-848-5134.
Credits: Impact America Foundation. 1991, 1993.
Recommended for Middle School, High School, and Adult.

Two survivors recount their experiences in Auschwitz after returning there with family members. Combined with historic footage, this is a moving commentary on prejudice. It also discusses Holocaust deniers. Teacher's guide available.

Night and Fog

D b/w 00:32:00

Source: Zenger Video, 10200 Jefferson Blvd., P.O. Box 802, Culver City, CA 90232-0802; 800-421-4246. #VY100V
Credits: Directed by Alain Resnais. 1955.
Recommended for Adult.

This award-winning, highly artistic documentary uses historic footage shot inside Nazi concentration camps and contrasts them with contemporary color scenes. The film includes very graphic footage. Attempting to universalize the Holocaust, the film never identifies the victims as Jews. In French, with English subtitles.

Triumph of Memory

D ST c 00:30:00

Source: PBS Video, 1320 Braddock Place, Alexandria, VA 22314-1698; 800-344-3337.
Credits: Produced and directed by Robert Gardner. Executive Producers, Sister Carol Rittner, R.S.M., and Sondra Myers. 1972.
Recommended for Middle School, High School, and Adult.

Non-Jewish resistance fighters sent to Nazi concentration camps bear witness to the atrocities that took place in Mauthausen, Buchenwald, and Auschwitz-Birkenau. This film is divided into three parts, which can be segmented for classroom use: initiation to the camps, daily life in the camps, and genocide. This is an excellent film for increased understanding of the Holocaust and life in the camps. It also includes a discussion of the victimization of Gypsies in the camp.

Resistance   ### Flames in the Ashes

D ST b/w 01:30:00

Source: Ergo Media, Inc., P.O. Box 2037, Teaneck, NJ 07666; 800-695-3746.
Credits: A Ghetto Fighters' House Release. Produced by Monia Avrahami. 1986.
Recommended for High School and Adult.

Historic, seldom seen footage tells the story of the variety of ways that Jews resisted the Nazis. Both murderers and resistance fighters tell the story. In Hebrew, Yiddish, French, Italian, and Polish, with subtitles.

Partisans of Vilna

D c b/w 02:10:00

Source: National Center for Jewish Film, Brandeis University, Lown 102, Waltham, MA 02254; 617-899-7044.
Credits: Produced by Aviva Kempner. Directed by Josh Waletzky. 1987.
Recommended for High School and Adult.

Featuring 40 interviews with survivors, this moving, informative film tells the story of Jewish resistance in the Vilna ghetto. Music sung in the ghetto and resistance, as well as interesting archival film footage, add greatly to the production. The film documents well the moral dilemmas and difficulties the resisters faced both inside the ghetto and later, in relations with non-Jews in partisan camps in the forests. It also shows the prominent role women played in the Vilna resistance. An important film best suited for more advanced students of the Holocaust. In Hebrew, Yiddish, and English, with subtitles.

Rescue   ***The Courage to Care***   D c b/w 00:28:00

Source: Zenger Video, 10200 Jefferson Blvd., P.O. Box 802, Culver City, CA 90232-0802; 800-421-4246. #ADL150V.
Credits: Produced and directed by Robert Gardner; Executive Producers, Sister Carol Rittner, R.S.M., and Sondra Meyers. 1986.
Recommended for Middle School, High School, and Adult.

> Nominated in 1986 for an Academy Award for best short documentary film, the film encounters ordinary people who refused to succumb to Nazi tyranny and reached out to help victims of the Holocaust.

The Other Side of Faith   D ST c 00:27:00

Source: Film and Video Foundation, 1800 K Street, N.W., Suite 1120, Washington, DC 20006; 202-429-9320.
Credits: Produced by Sy Rotter. 1990.
Recommended for Middle School, High School, and Adult.

> Filmed on location in Przemsyl, Poland, this first-person narrative tells of a courageous sixteen-year-old Catholic girl who, for two-and-a-half years, hid thirteen Jewish men, women, and children in the attic of her home.

Raoul Wallenberg: Between the Lines   D ST c b/w 01:25:00

Source: Zenger Video, 10200 Jefferson Blvd., P.O. Box 802, Culver City, CA 90232-0802; 800-421-4246. #SV996V.
Credits: Written and directed by Karin Altmann. 1985.
Recommended for High School and Adult.

> Raoul Wallenberg, a Swedish diplomat, was responsible for saving thousands of lives. Friends, family, and former members of his staff describe Wallenberg's efforts to confront the Nazi destruction of Hungarian Jewry. The video also examines the controversy surrounding his arrest and imprisonment in 1945 by the Soviets. Historic film footage is used.

Au Revoir Les Enfants (Goodbye, Children)   DD c 01:03:00

Source: Orion Home Video, 1888 Century Park East, Los Angeles, CA 90067; 310-282-2576
Credits: Produced and directed by Louis Malle. 1987.
Recommended for High School and Adult.

Based on Malle's own experiences in a French boarding school during the German occupation, this moving film documents the friendship between a 12-year-old Catholic boy and a Jewish youngster being sheltered at the school by a priest. The movie ends with the betrayal of the hidden child's identity to the Gestapo and his arrest, along with the priest. In French, with subtitles.

Schindler's List   DD b/w c 03:17:00

Source: Zenger Video, 10200 Jefferson Blvd., P.O. Box 802, Culver City, CA 90232-0802; 800-421-4246. #MCA172V-J5.
Credits: Directed by Steven Spielberg. Adapted from Thomas Keneally's fictionalized account of a true story. 1993.
Recommended for High School and Adult.

Shot on location in Poland in stark black-and-white, this compelling Oscar-winning film tells the story of German businessman Oskar Schindler who saved more than 1000 Jews from deportation and death. The book *Schindler's List* by Thomas Keneally chronicles the story more fully and with the greater nuance that a written account allows. Contains graphic violence, strong language, and nudity.

Weapons of the Spirit   D c 00:38:00

Source: Zenger Video, 10200 Jefferson Blvd., P.O. Box 802, Culver City, CA 90232-0802; 800-421-4246. #ADL156V.
Credits: Written, produced, and directed by Pierre Sauvage. 1988.
Recommended for Middle School, High School, and Adult.

This is the story of Le Chambon-sur-Lignon, a small Protestant village in south-central France, and how its predominantly Protestant citizens responded to the Nazi threat against the Jews. Residents of the area hid and cared for 5,000 Jews, many of them children.

Auschwitz and the Allies

D ST c b/w 01:53:00

Source: No distributor currently available.
Credits: B.B.C. Production. Martin Gilbert, Consultant. 1980.
Recommended for High School and Adult. Could be segmented for use in Middle School.

This film examines the responses of Allied governments as well as those of the International Red Cross, the Jewish community, and the victims. There are also many interviews with historic figures. This excellent film can be segmented for classroom use.

Safe Haven

D ST c 00:57:40

Source: No distributor currently available.
Credits: WXXI-TV, Rochester, NY. Produced and directed by Paul Lewis. 1987.
Recommended for Middle School, High School, and Adult.

Safe Haven tells the story of America's only refugee camp for victims of Nazi terror. Nearly 1,000 refugees were brought to Oswego, N.Y., and incarcerated in a camp known as Fort Ontario for eighteen months.

Who Shall Live and Who Shall Die?

D b/w 01:30:00

Source: Zenger Video, 10200 Jefferson Blvd., P.O. Box 802, Culver City, CA 90232-0802; 800-421-4246. #KN103V-J4.
Credits: Produced by James R. Kurth and Laurence Jarvik; directed by Laurence Jarvik. 1982.
Recommended for High School and Adult.

This film examines American responses to the Holocaust with particular attention to the actions (or failures to act) of American Jewish leaders. It is a detailed, informative presentation of a complex topic, with oral testimony from a wide range of Jews and non-Jews involved with the issue of Jewish rescue. Indispensable for more advanced students of the Holocaust. Graphic images.

America and the Holocaust: Deceit and Indifference   [D] [b/w] [c] 01:00:00

Source: PBS Video, 1320 Braddock Place, Alexandria, VA 22314-1698; 800-344-3337.
Credits: Produced by Marty Ostrow. 1994.
Recommended for High School and Adult.

This film focuses mostly on the responses of Roosevelt, the State Department, and other U.S. government leaders to the Nazis' persecution and mass murder of European Jews. Weaving together interviews, official photos and documents, home movies, and archival footage, the production is especially good at tracing the complex social and political factors that shaped American responses to the Holocaust. The history is interwoven with the moving personal story of Jewish refugee Kurt Klein, who failed in his efforts to obtain visas for his parents to follow him to the United States.

The Double Crossing: The Voyage of the St. Louis   [D] [b/w] [c] 00:29:00

Source: Zenger Video, 10200 Jefferson Blvd., P.O. Box 802, Culver City, CA 90232-0802. 800-421-4246. #ER110V-J4.
Credits: A production of the Holocaust Memorial Foundation of Illinois and Loyola University of Chicago. Produced by Elliot Lefkovitz and Nancy Partos, 1992.
Recommended for High School and Adult.

More than 900 Jewish refugees fleeing Nazi Germany in 1939 on the luxury cruise ship the SS *St. Louis* were denied entry to Cuba and the United States and forced to return to Europe. In interviews interwoven with archival footage and photos, surviving passengers relive their voyage. The general issues this highly recommended film addresses—racism, quota systems for refugees, and immigration policies—remain urgent ones today.

The Boat is Full   [DR] [b/w] 01:44:00

Source: Zenger Video, 10200 Jefferson Blvd., P.O. Box 802, Culver City, CA 90232-0802; 800-421-4246. #FJ100V-J4.
Credits: Produced by George Reinhart, Limbo Films, Inc., in coproduction with SRG, ZDF, ORF. Directed by Markus Imhoo. 1980.
Recommended for High School and Adult.

In 1942 the Swiss government, alarmed at the vast numbers of people fleeing Nazi Germany, established stringent immigration policies as they declared the country's "lifeboat" full. Nominated for an Academy Award for best foreign film, this suspenseful drama tells the story of a group of refugees forced back to the border by ordinary citizens too frightened or indifferent to take them in. In German, with English subtitles.

Liberation

Holocaust: Liberation of Auschwitz

D b/w c 00:18:00

Source: Zenger Video, 10200 Jefferson Blvd., P.O. Box 802, Culver City, CA 90232-0802; 800-421-4246. #EBE 296 V.
Credits: Encyclopedia Britannica. 1990.
Recommended for High School and Adult.

> The liberation of Auschwitz is filmed by Soviets, who linger on the faces of the inmates. Commentary describes the selection process, medical experiments, and daily life at Auschwitz. Soviet cameraman Alexander Vorontsov shares his impressions of the liberation. Highly graphic footage is included.

Liberation 1945: Testimony

D b/w c 01:16:00

Source: United States Holocaust Memorial Museum, 100 Raoul Wallenberg Place SW, Washington, DC 20024-2150; 202-488-6144.
Credits: Produced by Sandy Bradley, Wentworth Films, in association with the United States Holocaust Memorial Museum. 1995.

> This film includes expanded eyewitness testimony produced for the Museum's special exhibition *Liberation 1945*. Jewish survivors and Allied liberators recall how they felt at liberation and describe conditions inside the camps, including difficulties faced by medical relief teams working in the liberated camps. Survivors interned in displaced persons camps describe the organization of those camps and their efforts both to find surviving family members and, by marrying, to establish new families.

Opening the Gates of Hell

D b/w c 00:45:00

Source: Ergo Media Inc., P.O. Box 2037, Teaneck, NJ 07666; 800-695-3746.
Credits: Production of the Holocaust Memorial Foundation of Illinois and Loyola University of Chicago. Directed by Timothy Roberts. 1992.
Recommended for High School and Adult.

> American liberators of the Nazi concentration camps share their memories of what they saw. Interviews are effectively combined with historic photos and footage showing the camps that were liberated by Americans: Buchenwald, Nordhausen, Dachau, Landsberg, and Mauthausen. The video includes graphic footage.

Post-Holocaust   **The Last Sea**   D b/w 01:30:00

Source: Ergo Media Inc., P.O. Box 2037, Teaneck, NJ 07666; 800-695-3746.
Credits: A Ghetto Fighters' House Release. Film by Haim Gouri, Jacquot Ehrlich, and David Bergman. 1987.
Recommended for High School and Adult.

The dramatic story of the postwar Jewish exodus from Europe to Israel is told using historic film footage. Finding themselves without family or homes to return to, many chose to make the hazardous journey by truck, by train, on foot, and finally on overcrowded boats.

Murderers Among Us: The Simon Wiesenthal Story   DR c 02:57:55

Source: Zenger Video, 10200 Jefferson Blvd., P.O. Box 802, Culver City, CA 90232-0802; 800-421-4246. #WV117V.
Credits: HBO Pictures, Robert Cooper Production. Produced by John Kemeny and Robert Cooper. 1988.
Recommended for High School and Adult.

This is the true story of a Holocaust survivor who committed himself in the years after liberation to the task of hunting Nazis and bringing them to justice. This video can be effectively paired with the book *The Sunflower*. It is also useful for examining the response to the Holocaust in the postwar period.

Nazi War Crime Trials   D b/w 01:07:00

Source: Video Images, Box C, Sandy Hook, CT 06482; 800-243-0987.
Recommended for Middle School, High School, and Adult.

This vintage film made in 1945 uses newsreels and documentary footage to show the fate of Goering, Hess, Schacht, Streicher, Keitel, and other Nazis who were brought to trial after the war.

Related Films   **The Hangman**   A c 00:12:00

Source: CRM, 2215 Faraday, Suite F, Carlsbad, CA 92008; 800-421-0833.
Credits: Melrose Productions. 1964.
Recommended for Middle School and High School.

Animation is used to illustrate the poem by Maurice Ogden about a town in which the people are hanged one by one by a mysterious hangman while the town stands by rationalizing each victimization. This may be useful in introducing the subject of individual responsibility and the role of the bystander in the Holocaust.

Obedience

D | b/w | 00:45:00

Source: Penn State Audio-Visuals Service; 800-826-0132. Rent or purchase.
Credits: Produced by Stanley Milgram. 1962.
Recommended for Middle School and High School.

This documentary shows the experiment conducted at Yale University testing the willingness of people to follow orders which required inflicting pain on another. This film may be used to provoke discussions on morality and responsibility. It has been used effectively with films on the Nuremberg Trials or the trial of Adolf Eichman, where the standard defense was that the criminals had only been following orders.

The Wave

DR | c | 00:46:00

Source: Zenger Video, 10200 Jefferson Blvd., P.O. Box 802, Culver City, CA 90232-0802; 800-421-4246. #FLM252V
Credits: Embassy Films. 1984.
Recommended for Middle School and High School.

This film recreates a classroom experiment done by a high school teacher who set up strict rules and behavior codes in an effort to show how peer pressure, conformity, and loyalty could work in a classroom the same way they had in Nazi Germany. This film may be used together with lessons on the rise of Nazism.

The Forgotten Genocide

D | ST | b/w | c | CC | 00:28:00

Source: Atlantis Productions, 1252 La Granada Drive, Thousand Oaks, CA 91362; 805-495-2790.
Credits: Written, produced, and directed by J. Michael Hagopian, Ph.D. 1975.
Recommended for Middle School, High School, and Adult.

Nominated for an Emmy, this is a shortened version of *The Armenian Case,* which documents the Armenian genocide that took place during and after World War I. Personal narrative is included with historic photos and film footage.

United States
Holocaust
Memorial
Museum

For the Living   ▢D ▢c 01:00:00

Source: United States Holocaust Memorial Museum, 100 Raoul Wallenberg Place SW, Washington, DC 20024-2150; 202-488-6144.
Credits: Produced by WETA, Washington. 1993.
Recommended for High School and Adult.

This film documents the creation, design, and building of the United States Holocaust Memorial Museum in Washington, D.C. Combining archival film footage and photos with on-location scenes at former Nazi camps in Poland, the video shows how the Museum's exhibits tell the story of both victims and survivors of the Holocaust. This film works best as an orientation for visitors to the Museum.

Index of
Videotapes by
Title

FREQUENTLY ASKED QUESTIONS

The brief answers offered here are only meant as an introduction to the complex history of the Holocaust. Scholars have spent years writing and researching about these questions.

1. What was the Holocaust?

The Holocaust was the state-sponsored, systematic persecution and annihilation of European Jewry by Nazi Germany and its collaborators between 1933 and 1945. Jews were the primary victims—six million were murdered; Gypsies, the handicapped, and Poles were also targeted for destruction or decimation for racial, ethnic, or national reasons. Millions more, including homosexuals, Jehovah's Witnesses, Soviet prisoners of war, and political dissidents, also suffered grievous oppression and death under Nazi tyranny.

2. Who were the Nazis?

"Nazi" is a short term for the National Socialist German Workers Party, a right-wing political party formed in 1919 primarily by unemployed German veterans of World War I. Adolf Hitler became head of the party in 1921, and under his leadership the party eventually became a powerful political force in German elections by the early 1930s. The Nazi party ideology was strongly anti-Communist, antisemitic, racist, nationalistic, imperialistic, and militaristic.

In 1933, the Nazi Party assumed power in Germany, and Adolf Hitler was appointed Chancellor. He ended German democracy and severely restricted basic rights such as freedom of speech, press, and assembly. He established a brutal dictatorship through a reign of terror. This created an atmosphere of fear, distrust, and suspicion in which people betrayed their neighbors and which helped the Nazis to obtain the acquiescence of social institutions such as the civil service, the educational system, churches, the judiciary, industry, business, and other professions.

3. Why did the Nazis want to kill large numbers of innocent people?

The Nazis believed that Germans were "racially superior" and that there was a struggle for survival between them and "inferior races." Jews, Roma and Sinti (Gypsies), and the handicapped were seen as a serious biological threat to the purity of the "German (Aryan) Race" and therefore had to be "exterminated." The Nazis blamed the Jews for Germany's defeat in World War I, for its economic problems, and for the spread of Communist parties throughout Europe. Slavic peoples (Poles, Russians, and others) were also considered "inferior" and destined to serve as slave labor for their German masters. Communists, socialists, Jehovah's Witnesses, homosexuals, and Freemasons were persecuted, imprisoned, and often killed on political and behavioral (rather than racial) grounds. Sometimes the distinction was not very clear. Millions of Soviet prisoners of war perished from starvation, disease, and forced labor or were killed for racial or political reasons.

4. HOW DID THE NAZIS CARRY OUT THEIR POLICY OF GENOCIDE?

In the late 1930s the Nazis killed thousands of handicapped Germans by lethal injection and poisonous gas. After the German invasion of the Soviet Union in June 1941, mobile killing units following in the wake of the German Army began shooting massive numbers of Jews and Gypsies in open fields and ravines on the outskirts of conquered cities and towns. Eventually the Nazis created a more secluded and organized method of killing enormous numbers of civilians—six extermination centers were established in occupied Poland, where large-scale murder by gas and body disposal through cremation were conducted systematically. Victims were deported to these centers from German-occupied western Europe and from the ghettos in eastern Europe that the Nazis had established. In addition, millions died in the ghettos and concentration camps as a result of forced labor, starvation, exposure, brutality, disease, and execution.

5. HOW DID THE WORLD RESPOND TO THE HOLOCAUST?

The United States and Great Britain as well as other nations outside Nazi Europe received numerous press reports in the 1930s about the persecution of Jews. By 1942 the governments of the United States and Great Britain had confirmed reports about "the final solution"—Germany's intent to kill all the Jews of Europe. However, influenced by antisemitism and fear of a massive influx of refugees, neither country modified their refugee policies. Their stated intention to defeat Germany militarily took precedence over rescue efforts, and therefore no specific attempts to stop or slow the genocide were made until mounting pressure eventually forced the United States to undertake limited rescue efforts in 1944.

In Europe, rampant antisemitism incited citizens of many German-occupied countries to collaborate with the Nazis in their genocidal policies. There were, however, individuals and groups in every occupied nation who, at great personal risk, helped hide those targeted by the Nazis. One nation, Denmark, saved most of its Jews in a nighttime rescue operation in 1943 in which Jews were ferried in fishing boats to safety in neutral Sweden.

*Hitler reviews
35,000 SA troops.
Berlin, Germany.
February 20, 1936.*
(USHMM)

THE HOLOCAUST: A HISTORICAL SUMMARY

The Holocaust was the state-sponsored, systematic persecution and annihilation of European Jewry by Nazi Germany and its collaborators between 1933 and 1945. Jews were the primary victims—six million were murdered; Gypsies, the handicapped, and Poles were also targeted for destruction or decimation for racial, ethnic, or national reasons. Millions more, including homosexuals, Jehovah's Witnesses, Soviet prisoners of war, and political dissidents, also suffered grievous oppression and death under Nazi tyranny.

The concentration camp is most closely associated with the Holocaust and remains an enduring symbol of the Nazi regime. The first camps opened soon after the Nazis took power in January 1933; they continued as a basic part of Nazi rule until May 8, 1945, when the war, and the Nazi regime, ended.

The events of the Holocaust occurred in two main phases: 1933–1939 and 1939–1945.

I. 1933–1939

On January 30, 1933, Adolf Hitler was named Chancellor, the most powerful position in the German government, by the aged President Hindenburg, who hoped Hitler could lead the nation out of its grave political and economic crisis. Hitler was the leader of the right-wing National Socialist German Workers Party (called the "Nazi Party" for short); it was, by 1933, one of the strongest parties in Germany, even though—reflecting the country's multiparty system—the Nazis had only won a plurality of 33 percent of the votes in the 1932 elections to the German parliament (*Reichstag*).

Once in power, Hitler moved quickly to end German democracy. He convinced his cabinet to invoke emergency clauses of the Constitution that permitted the suspension of individual freedoms of press, speech, and assembly. Special security forces—the Special State Police (the Gestapo), the Storm Troopers (SA), and the Security Police (SS)—murdered or arrested leaders of opposition political parties (Communists, socialists, and liberals). The Enabling Act of March 23, 1933, forced through a Reichstag already purged of many political opponents, gave dictatorial powers to Hitler.

Also in 1933, the Nazis began to put into practice their racial ideology. Echoing ideas popular in Germany as well as most other western nations well before the 1930s, the Nazis believed that the Germans were "racially superior" and that

The boycott placard reads: "Germans! Defend yourselves! Do not buy from Jews!" Berlin, Germany. April 1, 1933.
(NARA)

there was a struggle for survival between them and "inferior races." They saw Jews, Roma (Gypsies), and the handicapped as a serious biological threat to the purity of the "German (Aryan[1]) Race," what they called the "master race."

Jews, who numbered nearly 600,000 in Germany (less than one percent of the total population in 1933), were the principal target of Nazi hatred. The Nazis mistakenly identified Jews as a race and defined this race as "inferior." They also spewed hate-mongering propaganda that unfairly blamed Jews for Germany's economic depression and the country's defeat in World War I (1914–1918).

In 1933, new German laws forced Jews to quit their civil service jobs, university and law court positions, and other areas of public life. In April 1933, a boycott of Jewish businesses was instituted. In 1935, laws proclaimed at Nuremberg made Jews second-class citizens. These "Nuremberg Laws" defined Jews not by their religion or by how they wanted to identify themselves but by the religious affiliation of their grandparents. Between 1937 and 1939, new anti-Jewish regulations segregated Jews further and made daily life very difficult for them: Jews could not attend public schools, go to theaters, cinemas, or vacation resorts, or reside, or even walk, in certain sections of German cities.

Also between 1937 and 1939, Jews were forced from Germany's economic life: the Nazis either seized Jewish businesses and properties outright or forced Jews to sell them at bargain prices. In November 1938, this economic attack against German and Austrian[2] Jews changed into the physical destruction of synagogues and Jewish-owned stores, the arrest of Jewish men, the destruction of homes, and the murder of individuals. This centrally organized riot (pogrom) became known as *Kristallnacht* (the "Night of Broken Glass").

Although Jews were the main target of Nazi hatred, the Nazis persecuted other groups they viewed as racially or genetically "inferior." Nazi racial ideology was buttressed by scientists who advocated "selective breeding" (eugenics) to "improve" the human race. Laws passed between 1933 and 1935 aimed to reduce the future number of genetic "inferiors" through involuntary sterilization programs:

1. The term "Aryan" originally referred to peoples speaking Indo-European languages. The Nazis perverted its meaning to support racist ideas by viewing those of Germanic background as prime examples of Aryan stock, which they considered racially superior. For the Nazis, the typical Aryan was blond, blue-eyed, and tall.

2. On March 11, 1938, Hitler sent his army into Austria, and on March 13 the incorporation (*Anschluss*) of Austria with the German empire (*Reich*) was proclaimed in Vienna. Most of the population welcomed the *Anschluss* and expressed their fervor in widespread riots and attacks against the Austrian Jews numbering 180,000 (90 percent of whom lived in Vienna).

Shop window of a Jewish-owned business destroyed during Kristallnacht. *Berlin, Germany. November 10, 1938.*
(NARA)

about 500 children of mixed (African-German) racial backgrounds[3] and 320,000 to 350,000 individuals judged physically or mentally handicapped were subjected to surgical or radiation procedures so they could not have children. Supporters of sterilization also argued that the handicapped burdened the community with the costs of their care. Many of Germany's 30,000 Gypsies were also eventually sterilized and prohibited, along with Blacks, from intermarrying with Germans. Reflecting traditional prejudices, new laws combined traditional prejudices with the new racism of the Nazis which defined Gypsies, by "race," as "criminal and asocial."

Another consequence of Hitler's ruthless dictatorship in the 1930s was the arrest of political opponents and trade unionists and others the Nazis labeled "undesirables" and "enemies of the state." Some five– to fifteen thousand homosexuals were imprisoned in concentration camps; under the 1935 Nazi-revised criminal code, the mere denunciation of a man as "homosexual" could result in arrest, trial, and conviction. Jehovah's Witnesses, who numbered 20,000 in Germany, were banned as an organization as early as April 1933, since the beliefs of this religious group prohibited them from swearing any oath to the state or serving in the German military. Their literature was confiscated, and they lost jobs, unemployment benefits, pensions, and all social welfare benefits. Many Witnesses were sent to prisons and concentration camps in Nazi Germany, and their children were sent to juvenile detention homes and orphanages.

Between 1933 and 1936, thousands of people, mostly political prisoners and Jehovah's Witnesses, were imprisoned in concentration camps, while several thousand German Gypsies were confined in special municipal camps. The first systematic round-ups of German and Austrian Jews occurred after *Kristallnacht*, when approximately 30,000 Jewish men were deported to Dachau and other concentration camps and several hundred Jewish women were sent to local jails. At the end of 1938, the waves of arrests also included several thousand German and Austrian Gypsies.

Between 1933 and 1939, about half the German Jewish population and more than two-thirds of Austrian Jews (1938–39) fled Nazi persecution. They emigrated mainly to Palestine, the United States, Latin America, Shanghai (which required no visa for entry), and eastern and western Europe (where many would be caught again in the Nazi net during the war). Jews who remained under Nazi rule

---

3. These children, called "the Rhineland bastards" by Germans, were the offspring of German women and African soldiers from French colonies who were stationed in the 1920s in the Rhineland, a demilitarized zone the Allies established after World War I as a buffer between Germany and western Europe.

Mass execution of Russian Jews by SS Einsatzgruppen *D. Vinnitsa, USSR. 1942.* (YIVO)

were either unwilling to uproot themselves or unable to obtain visas, sponsors in host countries, or funds for emigration. Most foreign countries, including the United States, Canada, Britain, and France, were unwilling to admit very large numbers of refugees.

II. 1939–1945

On September 1, 1939, Germany invaded Poland and World War II began. Within days, the Polish army was defeated, and the Nazis began their campaign to destroy Polish culture and enslave the Polish people, whom they viewed as "sub-human." Killing Polish leaders was the first step: German soldiers carried out massacres of university professors, artists, writers, politicians, and many Catholic priests. To create new living space for the "superior Germanic race," large segments of the Polish population were resettled, and German families moved into the emptied lands. Thousands of other Poles, including Jews, were imprisoned in concentration camps. The Nazis also "kidnapped" as many as 50,000 "Aryan-looking" Polish children from their parents and took them to Germany to be adopted by German families. Many of these children were later rejected as not capable of Germanization and sent to special children's camps, where some died of starvation, lethal injection, and disease.

As the war began in 1939, Hitler initialed an order to kill institutionalized, handicapped patients deemed "incurable." Special commissions of physicians reviewed questionnaires filled out by all state hospitals and then decided if a patient should be killed. The doomed were then transferred to six institutions in Germany and Austria, where specially constructed gas chambers were used to kill them. After public protests in 1941, the Nazi leadership continued this euphemistically termed "euthanasia" program in secret. Babies, small children, and other victims were thereafter killed by lethal injection and pills and by forced starvation.

The "euthanasia" program contained all the elements later required for mass murder of European Jews and Gypsies in Nazi death camps: an articulated decision to kill, specially trained personnel, the apparatus for killing by gas, and the use of euphemistic language like "euthanasia" that psychologically distanced the murderers from their victims and hid the criminal character of the killings from the public.

In 1940 German forces continued their conquest of much of Europe, easily defeating Denmark, Norway, the Netherlands, Belgium, Luxembourg, and France. On June 22, 1941, the German army invaded the Soviet Union and by September was

Inmates at forced labor in a concentration camp. Mauthausen, Austria. June–September 1942. (NARA)

approaching Moscow. In the meantime, Italy, Romania, and Hungary had joined the Axis powers led by Germany and opposed by the Allied Powers (British Commonwealth, Free France, the United States, and the Soviet Union).

In the months following Germany's invasion of the Soviet Union, Jews, political leaders, Communists, and many Gypsies were killed in mass executions. The overwhelming majority of those killed were Jews. These murders were carried out at improvised sites throughout the Soviet Union by members of mobile killing squads *(Einsatzgruppen)* who followed in the wake of the invading Germany army. The most famous of these sites was Babi Yar, near Kiev, where an estimated 33,000 persons, mostly Jews, were murdered. German terror extended to institutionalized handicapped and psychiatric patients in the Soviet Union; it also resulted in the mass murder of more than three million Soviet prisoners of war.

World War II brought major changes to the concentration camp system. Large numbers of new prisoners, deported from all German-occupied countries, now flooded the camps. Often entire groups were committed to the camps, such as members of underground resistance organizations who were rounded up in a sweep across western Europe under the 1941 "Night and Fog" decree. To accommodate the massive increase in the number of prisoners, hundreds of new camps were established in occupied territories of eastern and western Europe.

During the war, ghettos, transit camps, and forced labor camps, in addition to the concentration camps, were created by the Germans and their collaborators to imprison Jews, Gypsies, and other victims of racial and ethnic hatred as well as political opponents and resistance fighters. Following the invasion of Poland, three million Polish Jews were forced into approximately 400 newly established ghettos, where they were segregated from the rest of the population. Large numbers of Jews were also deported from other cities and countries, including Germany, to ghettos in Poland and German-occupied territories further east.

In Polish cities under Nazi occupation, like Warsaw and Lodz, Jews were confined in sealed ghettos where starvation, overcrowding, exposure to cold, and contagious diseases killed tens of thousands of people. In Warsaw and elsewhere, ghettoized Jews made every effort, often at great risk, to maintain their cultural, communal, and religious lives. The ghettos also provided a forced labor pool for the Germans, and many forced laborers (who worked on road gangs, in construction, or other hard labor related to the German war effort) died from exhaustion or maltreatment.

Between 1942 and 1944, the Germans moved to eliminate the ghettos in occupied Poland and elsewhere, deporting ghetto residents to "extermination camps"— killing centers equipped with gassing facilities—located in Poland. After the

German soldiers round up Jews during the Warsaw ghetto uprising. Warsaw, Poland. April 19–May 16, 1943. (NARA)

meeting of senior German government officials in late January 1942 at a villa in the Berlin suburb of Wannsee, the decision to implement "the final solution of the Jewish question" became formal state policy, and Jews from western Europe were also sent to killing centers in the East.

The six killing sites, chosen because of their closeness to rail lines and their location in semi-rural areas, were at Belzec, Sobibor, Treblinka, Chelmno, Majdanek, and Auschwitz-Birkenau. Chelmno was the first camp in which mass executions were carried out by gas, piped into mobile gas vans; 320,000 persons were killed there between December 1941 and March 1943 and between June to July 1944. A killing center using gas vans and later gas chambers operated at Belzec, where more than 600,000 persons were killed between May 1942 and August 1943. Sobibor opened in May 1942 and closed one day after a rebellion of the prisoners on October 14, 1943; up to 200,000 persons were killed by gassing. Treblinka opened in July 1942 and closed in November 1943; a revolt by the prisoners in early August 1943 destroyed much of the facility. At least 750,000 persons were killed at Treblinka, physically the largest of the killing centers. Almost all of the victims at Chelmno, Belzec, Sobibor, and Treblinka were Jews; a few were Gypsies. Very few individuals survived these four killing centers, where most victims were murdered immediately after arrival.

Auschwitz-Birkenau, which also served as a concentration camp and slave labor camp, became the killing center where the largest numbers of European Jews and Gypsies were killed. After an experimental gassing there in September 1941 of 250 malnourished and ill Polish prisoners and 600 Russian POWs, mass murder became a daily routine; more than 1.25 million people were killed at Auschwitz-Birkenau, 9 out of 10 of them Jews. In addition, Gypsies, Soviet POWs, and ill prisoners of all nationalities died in the gas chambers. Between May 14 and July 8, 1944, 437,402 Hungarian Jews were deported to Auschwitz in 48 trains. This was probably the largest single mass deportation during the Holocaust. A similar system was implemented at Majdanek, which also doubled as a concentration camp and where at least 275,000 persons were killed in the gas chambers or died from malnutrition, brutality, and disease.

The methods of murder were the same in all the killing centers, which were operated by the SS. The victims arrived in railroad freight cars and passenger trains, mostly from ghettos and camps in occupied Poland, but also from almost every other eastern and western European country. On arrival, men were separated from women and children. Prisoners were forced to undress and hand over all valuables. They were then driven naked into the gas chambers, which were disguised as shower rooms, and either carbon monoxide or Zyklon B (a form of

Prisoners from Dachau during a "death march." Gruenwald, Germany. April 29, 1945.
(YAD VASHEM)

crystalline prussic acid, also used as an insecticide in some camps) was used to asphyxiate them. The minority selected for forced labor were, after initial quarantine, vulnerable to malnutrition, exposure, epidemics, medical experiments, and brutality; many perished as a result.

The Germans carried out their systematic murderous activities with the active help of local collaborators in many countries and the acquiescence or indifference of millions of bystanders. However, there were instances of organized resistance. For example, in the fall of 1943, the Danish resistance, with the support of the local population, rescued nearly the entire Jewish community in Denmark from the threat of deportation to the east by smuggling them via a dramatic boatlift to safety in neutral Sweden. Individuals in many other countries also risked their lives to save Jews and other individuals subject to Nazi persecution. One of the most famous was Raoul Wallenberg, a Swedish diplomat who led the rescue effort that saved the lives of tens of thousands of Hungarian Jews in 1944.

Resistance movements existed in almost every concentration camp and ghetto of Europe. In addition to the armed revolts at Sobibor and Treblinka, Jewish resistance in the Warsaw ghetto led to a courageous uprising in April–May 1943, despite a predictable doomed outcome because of superior German force. In general, rescue or aid to Holocaust victims was not a priority of resistance organizations whose principal goal was to fight the war against the Germans. Nonetheless, such groups and Jewish partisans (resistance fighters) sometimes cooperated with each other to save Jews. On April 19, 1943, for instance, members of the National Committee for the Defense of Jews, in cooperation with Christian railroad workers and the general underground in Belgium, attacked a train leaving the Belgian transit camp of Malines headed for Auschwitz and succeeded in assisting several hundred Jewish deportees to escape.

After the war turned against Germany and the Allied armies approached German soil in late 1944, the SS decided to evacuate outlying concentration camps. The Germans tried to cover up the evidence of genocide and deported prisoners to camps inside Germany to prevent their liberation. Many inmates died during the long journeys on foot known as "death marches." During the final days, in the spring of 1945, conditions in the remaining concentration camps exacted a terrible toll in human lives. Even concentration camps never intended for extermination, such as Bergen-Belsen, became death traps for thousands, including Anne Frank, who died there of typhus in March 1945.

Former prisoners at the Allach subcamp of Dachau celebrate on April 30, 1945, the day after the camp's liberation.
(NARA)

In May 1945, Nazi Germany collapsed, the SS guards fled, and the camps ceased to exist as extermination, forced labor, or concentration camps. Some of the concentration camps, including Bergen-Belsen, Dachau, and Landsberg, all in Allied-occupied Germany, were turned into camps for displaced persons (DPs), which included former Holocaust victims unable to be repatriated.

The Nazi legacy was a vast empire of murder, pillage, and exploitation that had affected every country of occupied Europe. The toll in lives was enormous. The full magnitude, and the moral and ethical implications, of this tragic era are only now beginning to be understood more fully.

Avram Rosenthal, 5, and his brother Emanuel, 2, in the Kovno ghetto in German-occupied Lithuania. The children were murdered at Majdanek in March 1944. February 1944.
(USHMM)

A few of the 40,000 Polish children imprisoned in Auschwitz before being deported to Germany. July 1944.
(MCINC)

CHILDREN AND THE HOLOCAUST

Up to one-and-a-half million children were murdered by the Nazis and their collaborators between 1933 and 1945. The overwhelming majority of them were Jewish. Thousands of Roma (Gypsy) children, disabled children, and Polish children were also among the victims.

The deaths of these children were not accidental: they were the deliberate result of actions taken by the German government under the leadership of Chancellor Adolf Hitler. The children were killed in various ways. Many were shot; many more were asphyxiated with poisonous gas in concentration camps or subjected to lethal injections. Others perished from disease, starvation, exposure, torture, and/or severe physical exhaustion from slave labor. Still others died as a result of medical experiments conducted on them by German doctors in the camps.

During the Holocaust, children—ranging in age from infants to older teens—were, like their parents, persecuted and killed not for anything they had done. Rather, Hitler and the Nazi government believed that so-called "Aryan" Germans were a superior race. The Nazis labeled other people they considered inferior as "non-Aryans." People belonging to non-Aryan groups, including children, were targeted by the Nazis for elimination from German society. The Nazis killed children to create a biologically pure society.

Even children who fit the Aryan stereotype suffered at the hands of the Nazis during World War II. Non-Jewish children in occupied countries whose physical appearance fit the Nazi notion of a "master race" (fair skin, blond-haired, blue-eyed) were at times kidnapped from their homes and taken to Germany to be adopted by German families. As many as 50,000 Polish children alone may have been separated from their families in this manner. Some of these children were later rejected and sent to special children's camps where they died of starvation or as a result of the terrible living conditions within the camps. Others were killed by lethal injections at the concentration camps of Majdanek and Auschwitz.

The experiences of children who were victims of Nazi hatred varied widely. Factors such as age, gender, family wealth, and where a child lived affected their experiences under German domination. Generally, babies and younger children deported to ghettos and camps had almost no chance of surviving. Children in their teens, or younger children who looked more mature than their years, had a better chance of survival since they might be selected for slave labor rather than for death. Some teens participated in resistance activities as well.

Children who were victims of the Holocaust came from all over Europe. They had different languages, customs, and religious beliefs. Some came from wealthy families; others from poor homes. Many ended their schooling early to work in a craft or trade; others looked forward to continuing their education at the university level. Still, whatever their differences, they shared one commonality: by the 1930s, with the rise of the Nazis to power in Germany, they all became potential victims and their lives were forever changed.

Nazi Germany, 1933–39

Soon after the Nazis gained power in Germany, Jewish children found life increasingly difficult. Due to legislation prohibiting Jews from engaging in various professions, their parents lost jobs and businesses. As a result, many families were left with little money. Jewish children were not allowed to participate in sports and social activities with their "Aryan" classmates and neighbors. They could not go to museums, movies, public playgrounds, or even swimming pools. Even when they were permitted to go to school, teachers often treated them with scorn and encouraged their humiliation by other students. Frequently, Jewish students were subject to being taunted and teased, picked upon and beaten up. Eventually, Jewish and Gypsy children were expelled from German schools.

Gypsy children, like Jewish children, faced many hardships in Nazi Germany. Along with their parents, they were rounded up and forced to live behind barbed wire in special municipal internment camps under police guard. Beginning in 1938, Gypsy teenagers were arrested and sent to concentration camps.

Murder Under Cover of War

With the outbreak of World War II in September 1939, life became much harder for children all over Europe. European children of all backgrounds suffered because of the war, experiencing displacement, inadequate diets, the absence of fathers and brothers, loss of family members, trauma, and confusion. However, only certain groups of children were singled out for "extinction."

Wartime, Hitler suggested, "was the best time for the elimination of the incurably ill." Among the first victims of the Nazis were disabled persons, and children were not exempt. Many Germans, influenced by Nazi ideas, did not want to be reminded of individuals who did not measure up to their idealized concept of a "master race." The physically and mentally handicapped were viewed by the Nazis as unproductive to society, a threat to Aryan genetic purity, and ultimately unworthy of life. Beginning almost simultaneously with the start of World War II, a "euthanasia" program was authorized personally by Adolf Hitler to systematically murder disabled Germans. Like disabled adults, children with disabilities were either injected with lethal drugs or asphyxiated by inhaling carbon monoxide fumes pumped into sealed mobile vans and gas chambers. Medical doctors cooperated in these so-called "mercy killings" in six institutions, and secretly at other centers, in Germany. Though some were Jewish, most of the children murdered in this fashion were non-Jewish Germans.

With the onset of war, Jewish children in Germany suffered increasing deprivations. Nazi government officials confiscated many items of value from Jewish homes, including radios, telephones, cameras, and cars. Even more importantly, food rations were curtailed for Jews as were clothing ration cards. Jewish children felt more and more isolated. Similarly, as Germany conquered various European countries in their war effort—from Poland and parts of the Soviet Union in the east, to Denmark, Norway, Belgium, France, and the Netherlands in the west—more and more Jewish children came under German control and, with their parents, experienced persecution, forced separations, and very often, murder.

Throughout eastern Europe, Jewish families were forced to give up their homes and relocate into ghettos—restricted areas set up by the Nazis as "Jewish residential districts." Most of the ghettos were located in German-occupied Poland; most were established in the poorer, more dilapidated sections of towns and cities. Ghettos were fenced in, typically with barbed wire or brick walls. Entry and exit were by permit or pass only; like a prison, armed guards stood at gates. Families inside the ghettos lived under horrid conditions. Typically, many families would be crowded into a few rooms where there was little if any heat, food, or privacy. It was difficult to keep clean. Many people in the ghettos perished from malnutrition, starvation, exposure, and epidemics. Typhus, a contagious disease spread by body lice, was common, as was typhoid, spread through contaminated drinking water.

Some children managed to escape deportation to ghettos by going into hiding with their families or by hiding alone, aided by non-Jewish friends and neighbors. Children in hiding often took on a secret life, sometimes remaining in one room for months or even years. Some hid in woodpiles, attics, or barns; others were locked in cupboards or concealed closets, coming out infrequently and only at night. Boys had it more difficult, because they were circumcised and could therefore be identified.

Children were often forced to live lives independent of their families. Many children who found refuge with others outside the ghettos had to assume new identities and conform to local religious customs that were different from their own in order to survive. Some Jewish children managed to pass as Catholics and were hidden in Catholic schools, orphanages, and convents in countries across Europe.

Jews being marched to the railway station for deportation to a death camp. Krakow, Poland. 1941. (YIVO)

Everyday, children became orphaned and many had to take care of even younger children. In the ghettos of Warsaw and other cities, many orphans lived on the streets, begging for bread and food from others in the ghetto who likewise had little or none to spare. Exposed to severe weather, frostbite, disease, and starvation, these children did not survive for long. Many froze to death.

In order to survive, children had to be resourceful and make themselves useful. In Lodz, healthy children could survive by working. Small children in the largest ghetto in occupied Poland, Warsaw, sometimes helped smuggle food to their families and friends by crawling through narrow openings in the ghetto wall. They did so at considerable risk, as smugglers who were caught were severely punished.

DEPORTATION TO CONCENTRATION CAMPS

The Nazis started emptying the ghettos in 1942 and deporting the victims to concentration camps. Children were often the target of special round-ups for deportation to the camps. The victims were told they were being resettled in the "East." The journey to the camps was difficult for everyone. Jammed into rail cars until there was no room for anyone to move, young children were often thrown on top of other people. Suffocating heat in the summer and freezing cold in the winter made the deportation journey even more brutal. During the trip, which often lasted several days, there was no food except for what people managed to bring along. There were also no water or bathroom facilities and parents were powerless to defend their children.

Two concentration camps (Auschwitz-Birkenau and Majdanek) and four other camps (Chelmno, Sobibor, Belzec, and Treblinka) functioned as "killing centers." All were located near railroad lines in occupied Poland, and poison gas—either carbon monoxide or Zyklon B—was the primary weapon of murder. At Chelmno, Sobibor, Belzec, and Treblinka, nearly everyone was killed soon after arrival. At Auschwitz and Majdanek, individuals were "selected" to live or to die. Stronger, healthier people—including many teenagers—were often selected for slave labor, forced to work eleven-hour shifts with minimum provisions for clothing, food, and shelter. Some who survived the camp "selection" process were used for medical experiments by German physicians.

The great majority of people deported to killing centers did not survive. For those who did survive the selection process, children and adults alike, life in the camps presented new challenges, humiliations, and deprivations. One became a prisoner: clothing and all possessions were removed. Hair was shaved off. Ill-fitting

Inmates at Buchenwald concentration camp a few days after their liberation. Elie Wiesel lies seventh from left on the second tier of bunks. April 16, 1945.
(NARA)

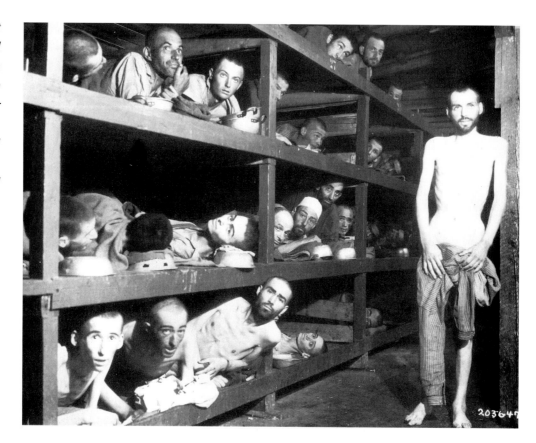

Wearing striped uniforms, inmates of Dachau stand at the formerly electrified fence to cheer as troops of the U.S. 7th Army approach. Dachau, Germany. April 29, 1945.
(NARA)

prison uniforms were distributed. One's name was replaced with a number often tattooed on the arm. Many people scarcely recognized their own family members after they had been processed in the camps.

Camp "inmates" were crowded into barracks fitted with wooden bunk beds stacked three or four on top of each other, and several people had to fit per level on the plank beds that had neither mattresses nor blankets. Lice were everywhere and contributed to the spread of disease, which was an ever-present enemy. Standing in roll calls for extended periods in all kinds of weather and working long hours took its toll on everyone. Daily rations of food consisted of a small piece of bread and coffee or soup. As a result of these brutal living conditions, many people died. Few lasted more than a month or two. Even among those that survived, one's vulnerability to "selection" had not ended at the point of arrival. The sick, the feeble, and those too exhausted to work were periodically identified and selected for gassing.

LIBERATION

Near the end of the war in 1945, the German concentration camps were liberated by Allied soldiers. By this time, many of the children who had entered camps as teenagers were now young adults. For most, the food and gestures of kindness offered by liberating soldiers were the links to life itself. Children who had survived in hiding now searched the camps trying to locate family members who might also have survived. Returning to hometowns, they had hopes that a former neighbor might know of other survivors.

It was rare for an entire family to survive the Holocaust. One or both parents were likely to have been killed; brothers and sisters had been lost; grandparents were dead. Anticipated reunions with family members gave surviving children some hope, but for many, the terrible reality was that they were now alone. Many found themselves sole survivors of once large extended families. A few were eventually able to locate missing family members.

Life as it had been before the Holocaust was forever altered. Though some individual survivors attempted to return to their former places of residence, Jewish and Gypsy communities no longer existed in most of Europe. Family homes had, in many instances, been taken over by others; personal possessions had been plundered. Because returning to one's home in hopes of reclaiming what had been lost was fraught with extreme danger, many young survivors eventually ended up instead in children's centers or displaced persons camps.

The future was as uncertain as the present was unstable. Many young people had had their schooling interrupted and could not easily resume their studies. Merely surviving took precedence over other concerns. Owning nothing and belonging nowhere, many children left Europe and, with assistance provided by immigrant aid societies or sponsorship from relatives abroad, they emigrated, usually to the United States, South Africa, and/or Palestine which, after 1948, became the State of Israel. There, in these newly adopted countries, they slowly developed new lives.

CHRONOLOGY

January 30, 1933
Adolf Hitler is appointed Chancellor of Germany.

February 28, 1933
German government takes away freedom of speech, assembly, press, and freedom from invasion of privacy (mail, telephone, telegraph) and from house search without warrant.

March 4, 1933
Franklin D. Roosevelt is inaugurated President of the United States.

March 20, 1933
First concentration camp opens at Dachau, Germany, for political opponents of the regime.

April 1, 1933
Nationwide boycott of Jewish-owned businesses in Germany is carried out under Nazi leadership.

April 7, 1933
Law excludes "non-Aryans" from government employment; Jewish civil servants, including university professors and schoolteachers, are fired in Germany.

May 10, 1933
Books written by Jews, political opponents of Nazis, and many others are burned during huge public rallies across Germany.

July 14, 1933
Law passed in Germany permitting the forced sterilization of Gypsies, the mentally and physically disabled, African-Germans, and others considered "inferior" or "unfit."

October 1934
First major wave of arrests of homosexuals occurs throughout Germany, continuing into November.

April 1935
Jehovah's Witnesses are banned from all civil service jobs and are arrested throughout Germany.

September 15, 1935
Citizenship and racial laws are announced at Nazi party rally in Nuremberg.

March 7, 1936
Hitler's army invades the Rhineland.

July 12, 1936
First German Gypsies are arrested and deported to Dachau concentration camp.

August 1–16, 1936
Olympic Games take place in Berlin. Anti-Jewish signs are removed until the Games are over.

March 13, 1938
Austria is annexed by Germany.

July 6–15, 1938
Representatives from thirty-two countries meet at Evian, France, to discuss refugee policies. Most of the countries refuse to let in more Jewish refugees.

November 9–10, 1938
Nazis burn synagogues and loot Jewish homes and businesses in nationwide pogroms called *Kristallnacht* ("Night of Broken Glass"). Nearly 30,000 German and Austrian Jewish men are deported to concentration camps. Many Jewish women are jailed.

November 15, 1938
All Jewish children are expelled from public schools. Segregated Jewish schools are created.

December 2–3, 1938
All Gypsies in the Reich are required to register with the police.

March 15, 1939
German troops invade Czechoslovakia.

June 1939
Cuba and the United States refuse to accept Jewish refugees aboard the ship S.S. *St. Louis*, which is forced to return to Europe.

September 1, 1939
Germany invades Poland; World War II begins.

October 1939
Hitler extends power of doctors to kill institutionalized mentally and physically disabled persons in the "euthanasia" program.

Spring 1940
Germany invades and defeats Denmark, Norway, Belgium, Luxembourg, the Netherlands, and France.

October 1940
Warsaw ghetto is established.

March 22, 1941
Gypsy and African-German children are expelled from public schools in the Reich.

March 24, 1941
Germany invades North Africa.

April 6, 1941
Germany invades Yugoslavia and Greece.

June 22, 1941
German army invades the Soviet Union. The *Einsatzgruppen*, mobile killing squads, begin mass murders of Jews, Gypsies, and Communist leaders.

September 23, 1941
Soviet prisoners of war and Polish prisoners are killed in Nazi test of gas chambers at Auschwitz in occupied Poland.

September 28–29, 1941
Nearly 34,000 Jews are murdered by mobile killing squads at Babi Yar, near Kiev (Ukraine).

October–November 1941
First group of German and Austrian Jews are deported to ghettos in eastern Europe.

December 7, 1941
Japan attacks Pearl Harbor.

December 8, 1941
Gassing operations begin at Chelmno "extermination" camp in occupied Poland.

December 11, 1941
Germany declares war on the United States.

January 20, 1942
Fifteen Nazi and government leaders meet at Wannsee, a section of Berlin, to discuss the "final solution to the Jewish question."

1942
Nazi "extermination" camps located in occupied Poland at Auschwitz-Birkenau, Treblinka, Sobibor, Belzec, and Majdanek-Lublin begin mass murder of Jews in gas chambers.

June 1, 1942
Jews in France and the Netherlands are required to wear identifying stars.

April 19–May 16, 1943
Jews in the Warsaw ghetto resist with arms the Germans' attempt to deport them to the Nazi extermination camps.

August 2, 1943
Inmates revolt at Treblinka.

Fall 1943
Danes use boats to smuggle most of the nation's Jews to neutral Sweden.

October 14, 1943
Inmates at Sobibor begin armed revolt.

January 1944
President Roosevelt sets up the War Refugee Board at the urging of Treasury Secretary Henry Morgenthau, Jr.

March 19, 1944
Germany occupies Hungary.

May 15–July 9, 1944
Over 430,000 Hungarian Jews are deported to Auschwitz-Birkenau, where most of them are gassed.

June 6, 1944
Allied powers invade western Europe on D-Day.

July 20, 1944
German officers fail in an attempt to assassinate Hitler.

July 23, 1944
Soviet troops arrive at Majdanek concentration camp.

August 2, 1944
Nazis destroy the Gypsy camp at Auschwitz-Birkenau; around 3,000 Gypsies are gassed.

October 7, 1944
Prisoners at Auschwitz-Birkenau revolt and blow up one crematorium.

January 17, 1945
Nazis evacuate Auschwitz; prisoners begin "death marches" toward Germany.

January 27, 1945
Soviet troops enter Auschwitz.

April 1945
U.S. troops liberate survivors at Buchenwald and Dachau concentration camps.

April 30, 1945
Hitler commits suicide in his bunker in Berlin.

May 5, 1945
U.S. troops liberate Mauthausen concentration camp.

May 7, 1945
Germany surrenders, and the war ends in Europe.

November 1945–October 1946
War crimes trials held at Nuremberg, Germany

May 14, 1948
State of Israel is established.